I0566915

"Pierre Teilhard de Chardin is an underappreciated spiritual master whose message is vital for our time. Christine Tracy's memoir of how Teilhard has inspired her life and work is thus a needed and welcome contribution to the ongoing re-discovery of Teilhard's teaching. For those who want to live out their spirituality, Christine's book will be an inspiration."

—Steve McIntosh, JD, author of *The Presence of the Infinite*

"The rawness and honesty with which Tracy reveals parts of her inner life in *Just Trust Life* is remarkable, as is the deep affection with which she talks about her relationship to the man, Teilhard, who died in the year of her birth. *Just Trust Life* is important reading for those who struggle with personal demons as well as those who have not yet come to understand Teilhard in the way Tracy has. The book will stay with me for a very long time. It made me a better version of myself."

—S. Michael Halloran, PhD, Professor Emeritus, Rensselaer Polytechnic Institute

Christine M. Tracy
Just Trust Life

Christine M. Tracy is a writer, journalist, and rhetorician. Inspired by the "noosphere," Teilhard's word for collective thought energy, Tracy coined the term "newsphere" and wrote *The Newsphere: Understanding the News and Information Environment* (Peter Lang 2012) to explain the paradox of the current news environment. She believes the energy of the noosphere can enhance collective evolution and wrote *The Mystic As Everyman* (Thought Catalog 2018) to help readers connect their "insides with their outsides." She is a member of the Council of Scholar Advisors for the Teilhard Project and has published scholarly essays exploring Teilhard's relationship to progressive disciplines, including media ecology and integral theory. She lives in Boulder, Colorado.

Just
Trust
Life

A Journey with Teilhard de Chardin

Christine M. Tracy

ISBN (paperback): 979-8-218-60039-6
ISBN (hardcover): 979-8-218-60340-3
ISBN (ebook): 979-8-218-60339-7

Library of Congress Control Number: 2025902743
Iphis Press: Boulder, Colorado

Cover and interior design by Raúl Peña (raulraul.com)
Author photo by Barbara Colombo

Copyright © 2025 by Christine M. Tracy

All rights reserved. Unauthorized duplication is a violation of applicable law. No part of this publication may be reproduced or transmitted in any form or by any means, electronic or mechanical, including photocopy, recording, or any information storage and retrieval system, without the express written permission of the author (except by a reviewer, who may quote brief passages and/or display brief passages in a short video clip, as a part of a professional review).

No generative artificial intelligence (AI) was used in the writing of this work. The author expressly prohibits any entity from using this publication to train AI technologies to generate text or for ML purposes, including, without limitation, technologies capable of generating textual or other works in the same style or genre as this publication.

Disclaimer: This book is a commentary on the spiritual and cosmological teachings and writings of the French Jesuit priest Pierre Teilhard de Chardin (1881–1955), and also comments on various books written about him. The author also discusses the application of his writings as applied to her life experiences. The author's opinions, comments, and criticisms may not be universally applicable to all people in all circumstances. The events, places, and conversations in this book are the recollections of the author that have been recreated from memory and/or supplemented and/or condensed, and/or omitted. It is acknowledged that some people may have memories of certain events that differ. The information presented in this book is intended as commentary and criticism and as general information for educational purposes only.

To my grandchildren

Embrace the all and manifest ease

Just
Trust
Life

Prologue

I LOOKED DOWN AS the heels of my black Pappagallo sandals sank a little deeper into the soft grass, and stole a glance at my watch. My head was bowed just low enough to appear respectful, but high enough so that I wouldn't miss the conclusion of the praying that signaled the continuation of the tour. It was a moment of communion with my companions whose eyes were keenly focused on the small white headstone with a neat etching:

P. PETRUS TEILHARD DE CHARDIN, S.J.

It was the spring of 1985. I was thirty years old and was born in 1955, the year Pierre Teilhard de Chardin died. On this sunny day, I was hosting a well-dressed couple from France who asked me in broken English to take them to the Jesuit cemetery—a quiet, obscure glen neatly tucked a few hundred yards beyond the Culinary Institute of America's main parking lot.

I had been working as a press aide at the Institute for almost a year and these requests to "see Teilhard's grave" were becoming routine.

Before it became the famous cooking school, the Culinary Institute's 170-acre Hyde Park campus was St. Andrew-on-Hudson, a Jesuit novitiate on the Hudson River just north of Poughkeepsie, New York. The headstones of the Jesuits interred there are lined up in neat, tidy rows. Teilhard's grave is distinctive because of regular cleaning and seasonal plantings, unlike his other Jesuit brothers who rest in obscurity.

"How many people come here to visit Teilhard's grave?" I asked the guard earlier that morning when I went to the Institute's security office to get the key that unlocked the gate to the cemetery.

"Oh, we get one or two people every day," he said.

I was surprised and intrigued. Although I went to a Catholic grammar school, high school, and college, I had never once heard Teilhard's name. How did so many people know he was buried here? I was curious about the Teilhard devotees who regularly found his humble grave on the big, bustling campus where white toques, checkered pants, and boxes of knives prevailed.

Years later, I understand their devotion. I now know that we are here to evolve and bravely trust our knowing, to use sacrifice and suffering as well as joy and ease with intention. This is our superpower.

Thirty-year-old me believed the answer to life's mysteries was in a book, in a psychiatrist's office, or in a bottle. In living my life, I have discovered that everything that happens to us—especially the things we label as "bad"—comes into our lives to bring us closer to the truth of who we really are. "We are not human beings having a spiritual experience. We are spiritual beings having a human experience," Teilhard said, according to folk wisdom.

In these pages, I will tell you how I came to live this truth.

One

All around us, tangibly and materially, the thinking envelope of the Earth—the Noosphere—is adding to its internal fibers and tightening its network; and at the same time its internal temperature is rising, and with this its psychic potential.

—Pierre Teilhard de Chardin, *The Future of Man*

I **SAT AND STARED** at the rainbows of light pouring from the multicolored stained-glass windows onto the floor of the Voorhees Computing Center. An air of the miraculous still permeated the space that was once a Catholic church. The pews and kneelers were replaced by computer monitors and screens, but the sense of devotion and solemnity remained.

I shifted my gaze from the mesmerizing light to the computer monitor in front of me and clumsily wove my way through the Unix directory structure as I looked for my assignment. I was an editor for *Computer-Mediated Communication Magazine* (CMC), and in February of 1997, my job was to edit Philip J. Cunningham's article "Teilhard de Chardin and the Noosphere" for the March issue.

I sat up a little straighter in my chair.

More than ten years after I had discovered a Frenchman's grave that attracted international visitors to the Culinary Institute of America's campus, I was encountering that Teilhard fellow again. It was the perfect opportunity to learn more about the mysterious Jesuit unpretentiously buried next to his brothers.

After my first visit to his grave, I had sensed that there was something extraordinary about Pierre Teilhard. But while I returned home and read some of the Culinary Institute's biographical materials, I promptly returned to my life. I was mildly curious, but not enough to continue exploring when motherhood demanded so much of my focus.

That was more than ten years ago. Now I was paying close attention. It was 1997 and I was in a master's program at Rensselaer Polytechnic Institute (RPI) in Troy, New York, where I had joined a small group of graduate students to produce *CMC*, one of the internet's first electronic magazines. John December, a prescient doctoral student, was its creator. As an early adopter, he understood the potential of the internet and its World Wide Web. He created a directory page for the web's newcomers (those were the days before the introduction of Mosaic, the first internet browser that could display text, graphics, and multimedia). John's page attracted so many hits that it slowed down the university's entire computer system.

I was confident of my editing ability, but intimidated by computing technologies: I am a "right-brainer" comfortable with abstract concepts, not a "left-brainer" who processes analytically. Learning to hand-code HTML, the hypertext markup language that made the web work, and navigate the Unix directory structure was a great challenge.

Whenever I approached the help desk with a question, a staff member calmly responded by asking me another question. I just wanted someone to come to my terminal, look over my shoulder and say, "Here's how you do this. Watch. I'll show you."

That never happened.

I hacked my way through as best I could and stood in awe of those who could program in seven different languages and otherwise master the new technological wizardry. My novice skills were sufficient to be named an editor of CMC, and as I sat hunched over my computer screen and struggled with the clunky interface of vi, the Unix text editor, I marveled at what was unfolding before me.

I grew up in Clark, New Jersey, thirty miles from Manhattan, and was a child of newspapers. My family subscribed to two dailies: The Newark *Star-Ledger* arrived early in the day and the Elizabeth *Daily Journal* in the afternoon. The papers sat on the coffee table waiting for my father to come home from work, and after he read both, it was my turn.

Later, as an undergraduate at Villanova University, I interned at the Norristown *Times Herald* in Norristown, Pennsylvania, where the air smelled like ink, precise lines of metal type were carefully placed in large wooden boxes, and big presses rolled over them to print the newspaper.

Everything was different now.

I could see it. I was living it. A handful of graduate students with only the investment of their time and talent were producing a monthly magazine that was distributed globally as soon as we hit the send button.

Truly heady stuff.

I leaned back in my rolling chair on that sunny afternoon in February and smiled in satisfaction as I closed my eyes. I let the perfume of industry and innovation that surrounded me seep into my bones.

Much like the seismic shifts in technology I was witnessing, I sensed that I was changing too. Like a swift-moving river rushing downstream, something was carrying me forward. I knew my life would be different, but I couldn't yet see how.

I was almost forty and my life had followed a predictable path: college, marriage, career, children, and now graduate school. I believed in working hard and vowed to live my conviction.

As I read Cunningham's piece about Teilhard, I encountered the word "noosphere" for the first time. My curiosity was aroused as I awkwardly toggled between screens trying not to lose my work. Working with his scientist friends, the Russian Vladimir Vernadsky and the Frenchman Édouard Le Roy, Teilhard coined the word "noosphere" in 1922 to describe an invisible "thinking layer" above the earth's physical biosphere.

Teilhard believed that the noosphere held the interior life of humanity: the thoughts, feelings, and emotions of humans, their consciousness. Like a dance, he saw these two forces—the insides and outsides, the noosphere and the biosphere—working together to evolve the earth.

I slowly began to understand Teilhard's teachings and beliefs and appreciate why people regularly visited his grave. I learned that Teilhard's personal faith was severely challenged during WWI, the infamous "war to end all wars," which injured or killed more than forty million people. In order to understand and learn to live with this human tragedy, he envisioned a cosmology that combined both his religious beliefs and his scientific knowledge.

I discovered that Teilhard was many things—a Jesuit priest, a paleontologist, a war hero, a cosmologist, and a philosopher—but what captured my imagination most was his insight and his almost magical ability to not only overcome obstacles, but to propel himself forward as well.

I was now looking at Teilhard through the eyes of a graduate student, which meant reading his writing and learning about his life. I didn't understand my attraction then—what some of my friends would later call an ob-session—but in my gut, I knew he had something fig-ured out that would help me live my life. Cunningham's article offered just enough biographical information sprinkled with theology for me to see the technological changes I was witnessing in a new way.

As I learned about his life, I discovered that this Jesuit priest and scientist was resilient, kind, beloved, courageous, intelligent—all the qualities I admired. But most of all, he understood energy. He believed the earth was a living organism and that it evolved through the collective thoughts, desires, motivations, and beliefs of humanity in a space he called the noosphere.

When Cunningham described Teilhard's vision of the noosphere, he said, "One cannot but think of today's Internet." Teilhard understood that technology could connect people in a way that was just then being explored by networked computing novices like me.

From that point on, I was forever captivated. Since Teilhard died in 1955, he probably saw an early television set and relied on radio. How could he have foreseen the vast improvements in our ability to communicate?

Almost a century later, here is this wireless, seamless web of connections: the internet, a real-life manifestation of that vision. Some called him the prophet of the internet, and from my place in the quiet serenity of the Voorhees Computing Center, where a chorus of keyboard strokes replaced the melodic chanting of a church choir, a seed was planted. I wanted to understand what he had believed: Did this unity of souls exist, and could humanity harness its power?

He eloquently shared this vision of a "supreme energy—the magnified equivalent of our intelligence and our will" in 1932 when he said mass in the shadow of China's Tian Shan mountains. Where did this innovative vision come from? How did this World War I chaplain, a stretcher-bearer who spent his childhood playing in the volcanic hills of the Auvergne region of France, this priest-scientist who watched the war brutalize his homeland, find not only optimism but a practical cosmology?

I needed to know, and so I began my long and continuing journey to understand the writings and life of this enigmatic philosopher who wrote, "The center of perspective, we are at the same time the *center of construction* of the universe." I didn't understand the question then. The joy and pain of my life would bring me the answer, but I did know that I wanted what Teilhard had—a deep and organic understanding that all is for our highest good, and with each step, and especially misstep, we are being led to something higher and more expansive.

Two

By virtue of the biological quality and properties
of thought, we find ourselves placed at a singular point,
at a node that commands the entire fraction of
the cosmos open to our experience at the present time.
The center of perspective, we are at the same
time the center of construction of the universe.

—Pierre Teilhard de Chardin, *The Human Phenomenon*

I TOOK MY SEAT IN THE second row of the small, shabby classroom and stared at the dirty tan shade on the big wooden windows in what was affectionately known as the "green roof" part of the Rensselaer campus. I took a notebook out of the green canvas L.L.Bean briefcase that my husband bought me as a gift when I entered the doctoral program eighteen months earlier. As I stuck the briefcase under my desk, I realized that the joy I felt back then was now a fleeting memory.

Joy. Who felt joy?

I was comfortably numb.

I had drunk just enough wine before I left the house to get me through Professor Halloran's Rhetoric of Nature and the Environment class, which lasted about two hours. As I sat waiting for the class to start, I thought about the customary stop I would make on the drive home. After class, I would walk to the parking lot and begin the twenty-minute drive home. Before I got there, I would stop at the liquor store on 146A near what the neighborhood kids called "the ghetto Chopper," buy a small four-pack of wine, and drink it in the car.

But class hadn't even started yet: I reminded myself that I could make it through before my ritual stop at the liquor store. My friend Virginia sat in front of me, and I studied her ease, grace, and beauty. We traveled together and shared rooms at academic conferences. She had introduced me to the neti pot and meditation. She was a good friend, but I couldn't stop comparing myself to her. She was all I wanted to be: thin, smartly dressed, cheerful, optimistic.

Instead of stylish jeans and a crisp white blouse like Virginia's, the contours of my body were hidden underneath a black and white silk muumuu dress; it was expensive and the fabric was lovely, but I felt frumpy as a haze of alcohol swirled inside me and filled my brain.

I used the time before Professor Halloran arrived to

intensify my self-hatred. Another good-looking student sat next to Virginia. More long blond hair, comfort, ease.

But it wasn't the hair. I grew up blond and could afford to highlight my own, so my New York State driver's license accurately said "Blond."

No, it was instead their self-confidence, contentment, intelligence, and perfume of power I envied. The closer I got to these women and the more they allowed me access to their inner sanctums, the more I contrasted them to my own perceived shortcomings.

Shortcomings is too weak a word.

I felt broken, hollow, an abject failure, an impostor. That's it.

I was an impostor. I was forty-six years old and simply not worthy to be a doctoral student in Professor Halloran's rhetoric classes at this technological university that was once headed by George M. Low, a Rensselaer alumnus, Presidential Medal of Freedom Recipient, and NASA star who helped to put a man on the moon. In a 1975 campus speech before he became the university's president, Low described the important lessons he learned as a Rensselaer student: "I learned how to be inquisitive. I learned to be curious. I learned not to be afraid to ask questions."

I felt like a polar opposite to Low: ashamed, hidden, silent in my suffering. How did I get here? And on a full scholarship, too? The answers eluded me, so I stayed anesthetized by alcohol and found a destructive pleasure in using these thoughts to widen the distance between myself and my classmates—the chosen ones who radiated inner peace and just plain-old liked and believed in themselves.

Always, always feeling less than.

Years later, I can see that I was trying harder and harder to be good enough, even though somewhere out there, like a distant star in the sky, there was the knowing that I was already okay—in fact, better than okay. I was the beautiful and divine "center of construction of the universe" that Teilhard envisioned.

What a thought!

But in 2001, I wasn't yet sober. I was drinking three or four glasses of wine every night, and somehow found time to read Teilhard's *Divine Milieu*, the poetic opus he composed after the war. Teilhard's words pulled my imagination in a new direction and felt like a flashlight in a storm. I sensed glimmers of a higher, brighter, more hopeful reality in his words. But that force wasn't yet strong enough to wake me up, to save me. And at that point, I did need saving.

I didn't quite have the language then: I was still speaking and thinking in graduate-student-talk and the language of denial. But I was, in fact, close to my bottom. In recovery-talk, a "bottom" is the place one reaches when the spiritual, emotional, and physical pain of pouring alcohol into one's body becomes too much.

What I didn't know then was that the same forces that saved Teilhard would save me. I was in a storm without a life jacket, but I would ultimately not drown.

I could see Teilhard in my mind, leaning over the casket of his beloved older brother, Alberic, who died of tuberculosis in 1902. Two years later, Teilhard lost his younger sister, Louise.

Profound grief precipitated a deep personal crisis in twenty-three-year-old Teilhard, and he considered abandoning his scientific studies to retreat into religious life. His mentor and friend, Paul Troussard, convinced him that he did not have to choose between paleontology and the priesthood: A divinely guided synthesis was possible. It was this momentous decision that forever altered his destiny.

Rays of my own personal synthesis were dawning inside me; I was beginning to see that it was safe to be my authentic self in the world. The doctoral program was buoyant protection in a storm, a safe place to focus my energy and retreat from my current stresses: raising my teenage boys, losing both my parents within months of each other, and feeling alone and isolated in important relationships.

Reflecting on the decisions Teilhard made helped me find the courage and strength to face my own truths.

But first I had to quit drinking.

I thought about stopping a lot: It played like a low hum inside, distracting and distancing me from whatever I was doing.

ॐ

I snapped out of my morbid reverie and started paying attention to Professor Halloran's lecture. I would find just the right opportunity to interject a thought that showed I had done the reading and was *mostly* following the discussion that day.

I had my say and then I was silent.

A few weeks later, a series of events unfolded that would forever change my life. It all began when I blacked out at a dinner given in honor of a distinguished campus visitor and was driven home by a kind graduate student, as a professor followed in my car.

When I awoke the next morning, my first thought was to get to the liquor store. My husband hid my car keys, so I got on my fancy ten speed Cannondale bicycle. I rode to the end of the driveway, fell over, and broke my collarbone.

The pain did not equal childbirth, but it was close. Each time I moved, a shot of hot, white light traveled through my body. And in some crazy way, I thought I deserved it; it was my body's way to telling me it was done with my drinking.

I don't know where I got the guts to get out of my pajamas, go to campus, and teach my 10:30 a.m. Writing To The Web class the next day. But I did: I faced the consequences of my excessive drinking, and it was excruciating. Small glimmers of light had broken through the illusory power of denial. And then pain, perhaps the greatest of all teachers, had shown up to give me the final lesson.

That morning, I couldn't drive, so my husband took time off from work to drive Mike and me to campus. With my arm in a navy-blue sling, I made the familiar long, steep climb from Eighth Street to Rensselaer's Russell Sage Laboratory, but this journey was very different.

Deep humiliation weighed on me with each step.

But I was done.

I carefully climbed the stairs to my classroom with my thirteen-year-old son Mike slowly, quietly walking behind me. He had stayed home from school so he could come with me and carry my briefcase and books.

Having him with me was both a comfort and a curse—a vivid example of my failure as a mother. I looked back and saw his bent head focusing on the cement steps. His short blond hair was neatly combed and guaranteed to stay in place with lots of hair gel. He wore his teenage uniform: a blue plaid button-down shirt, khaki cargo shorts, and white high-top sneakers.

He caught my eye and offered a small smile. I imagined that same mixture of relief and humiliation that swirled inside of me had pulled him into our family vortex of alcoholism. This was the same little boy who sat perched on my knee and celebrated Mother's Day at a kindergarten luncheon. I held him close as we posed for pictures. I was wearing a green-striped pants suit, and he had on the green sweater his grandparents brought back from Ireland. In a mysterious way, our clothing matched, and the joy and love we felt for each other shone as we smiled at the camera.

I needed moments like those to remind me of who I really was, so I could show up and teach that day.

Mike sat down in the last row of the big classroom and played computer games while I taught the seventy-five-minute class. I walked up to the front of the room and stood before the eight students enrolled in my class.

"How did you hurt your arm?" a student asked.

Eventually, I would tell the whole truth and nothing but the truth. But that morning in class, I could only share a partial truth with my students. I repeated the mantra: "I fell off my bicycle. I didn't clip out of the pedals in time, fell over, and broke my collarbone."

The students stared in disbelief. I knew I looked like shit.

Silence.

I took a deep breath and started the lecture.

When I went deep down past the pain and touched that place of true knowing, the seat of the internal navigation that saves us if we let it, I understood that I was doing all of this to myself.

Months later, as the fog in my brain began to clear, I realized I needed both extraordinary physical and unbearable emotional pain to touch that place inside me that alcohol numbed for so many years.

It's simple really. The pain just got to be too much, and I finally gave up. I made the choice to reenter reality.

As I learned more and more about Teilhard's life and studied his teachings, I realized I did not have to look outside myself for transcendence.

❧

Along with all the books I read during my doctoral work, I began collecting biographies of Teilhard—Ursula King's *Spirit of Fire* and Claude Cuenot's *Teilhard de Chardin* were favorites. In my excruciating process of finally getting sober, I thought about the inner truth that propelled Teilhard to remain in the Church after being silenced by his superiors.

Repeated petitions for permission to publish his progressive ideas were consistently denied by Church authorities, who saw the popular Jesuit as a threat to existing dogma. A "crisis of obedience," as Teilhard biographer Robert Speaight called it, occurred when "in 1928, a Jesuit traveled to Paris to warn Teilhard again that unless he changed his ways, he would be banished to an even more remote location than China, and would not be allowed to continue his scientific work."

The choice wasn't easy. Teilhard wrote to his friend Auguste Valensin that he sometimes felt like "a bird being whirled about in a great wind." He ultimately decided to "swallow the obstacle in the act of my obedience."

Inspired by the events from Teilhard's life, I found the courage to break through my denial and to finally put down alcohol. I began to trust my own interiority, my chi, the force that animated me. Like blowing up a balloon, I felt a growing expansiveness deep within my gut. It pushed outward and started to fill me up inside.

It pushed outward and started to fill me up inside.

Two

It all became crystal clear: I was doing it.
No one else.
It was me.
I was responsible for destroying my body, my life,
my soul. I was doing it to myself, and I could stop.
I had a choice.
Then, at age forty-six, I chose to stop drinking.

Three

One could say that the whole of life lies in seeing ...
To try to see more and to see better is not,
therefore, just a fantasy, curiosity, or a luxury. See
or perish ... this is the human condition.

—Pierre Teilhard de Chardin, *The Human Phenomenon*

I PICKED UP THE PHONE and heard her voice.

Instead of dwelling on the rising current of anger, sadness, and heartache that swelled up within me, I focused on the weeping willow tree in the front yard. When reflected in the early afternoon light, its long branches looked like the folds of a blanket.

It was springtime in upstate New York and leaves clothed the willow. The tree had been a good friend for the fifteen years I lived in the sprawling development just north of Albany.

Like a bird, I often sat perched on the brick fence surrounding the front walk and listened as my friend swayed in the wind and sang me a sweet song.

It was a low-pitched murmur. Faint. But I could hear it.

A secret message. The clandestine language we shared. I thanked her for the times she held my young sons when they climbed her low branches and sat contentedly in the crux of her outstretched arms.

The willow was the best part of the property that ultimately became "the marital residence." On that pivotal day, and indeed every day, she stood steady: gently moved by the breeze but unwavering in the deep rootedness of her resolve.

I looked at her, met her gaze, and I resolved too.

I resolved not to cry.

It was 2002, and I was six months sober. Bright-eyed. Clear-minded. I had stopped drinking. My mind and body were healing. It was and still is one of the best choices I ever made.

I had been self-medicating for a long time. Alcohol rewired my brain so drinking felt like the only option for coping with my confusion and turbulent emotions.

It was time to take responsibility.

Now that I was sober, I could no longer blame the actions, events, and people around me for my alcohol abuse.

A life lesson soon appeared. I picked up the phone to make a call and heard her melodious, seductive voice.

I was in my garage with my teenage son Mike, who was earning money from selling his old sweatshirts, pajamas, books, and soccer balls to buy a new video game system. He was standing a few feet from me and noticed my silence.

"Mom, Mom, are you okay?" Mike asked with a hint of fear in his voice. "Who are you talking to?"

I didn't answer him, so he asked again. "Mom, Mom, answer me! Who are you talking to?" Mike insisted with urgency.

"I'm listening to a voicemail message," I told him finally, which was indeed true. With my newly minted sobriety came a vow of honesty, which I swore to uphold.

"I am listening to a voicemail message," I said again. But I did leave out the rest of the details. I guess that was really lying by omission, which was still lying. But he was only fourteen years old, and I wanted to protect him.

As I listened to her enticing voice, there was no longer any doubt in my mind about my husband's infidelity. I moved between calm, anger, and sorrow like a balloon flapping in the breeze. Was I even still in love with him?

Or was my suburban life so demanding and distracting that I hadn't even considered the question?

What I do know is that a part of me was relieved. That may sound crazy, but the wife-me who didn't like her husband anymore, who couldn't stand the way he dressed, who used alcohol to lubricate sex, was surprisingly grateful. The wife-me let out a big sigh.

But the woman-me was outraged. "How could you cheat on me? Me? I am allowed to not want you (and perhaps I hadn't for a long time). But not wanting me isn't allowed."

My ego singed in agony.

"I can leave you, but you can't leave me."

It hurt to be rejected and to become the "leavee." I had the fancy degree. I was smart. I should have seen it coming.

But I didn't.

I didn't know.

Other people's husbands cheated on them. I held their hands; I gave them money to hire a lawyer; I called the "other woman's" place of employment to find out if she was there that day, or if she was, as suspected, on a romantic getaway with her lover, a.k.a. my friend's husband.

Now it was my turn to taste the toxic cocktail of betrayal, and there was no turning back. It was the stuff of Greek tragedies and Shakespearean plays. The hypnotic swirl of shock, rage, and embarrassment filled my insides.

The truth came barreling at me like a moving train. I barely heard her words, but I felt the connection between them. The snippets of conversation receded into the background: All I heard was her sexy voice. It felt like a magnet, and what unnerved me most wasn't the words she spoke, but the intimacy I now knew they shared.

Did Teilhard feel like he was going crazy when his gut told him to dig and keep digging before he unearthed an amazing fossil, an important piece of the puzzle that helped explain humanity's history on the planet? Was this the awareness he so often demonstrated in his life?

What stares us in the face is often the most difficult to perceive, Teilhard advised.

I had sensed something was wrong and had been trying to understand the dramatic change in my husband's behavior: the Friday night retirement dinners, new clothing purchases, golf outings, Sunday shopping trips, constant exercising. It now all made sense: My husband was having an affair.

I now had proof.

My husband of twenty-three years was in love with someone else.

My body and mind were frozen as I stood in the dusty and dirty garage listening to her words flow like well-aged wine.

There was no shouting. No angry scene in front of our teenage son, who was excited that the proceeds from his sale had netted enough money for the new video game system he coveted.

Perhaps there wasn't enough love left to generate anger and rage over the end of our long marriage.

I'll never know.

My sons went the way of young boys on a Saturday night. I took a shower, put on my best sundress, and went food shopping. If I looked good, I reasoned, my ego would be momentarily soothed. "You look good. That's all that matters," I said to my reflection in the mirror, trying to convince myself of that hollow fact.

But my indignation smoldered as I lay in bed that night and struggled with the choices I faced. Like vomit traveling from my stomach to my mouth, a need for revenge consumed me. The ferocious desire to shed my own pain and inflict it on someone else engulfed me, and I began planning how I would tell her husband.

"You don't want to destroy two more lives," was my husband's response when I told him my plan to contact her spouse.

"My life's not destroyed," I said. The words bypassed my brain and came from deep inside me.

It was a crazy paradox: Comfort came not from what I was wearing or anything on the outside. It came from my insides: Like a bucket traveling down a deep and dark well, I touched a place beyond betrayal, confusion, and fear. My pain pushed me to the doorway of authentic knowing.

This is my superpower.

Four

... the front cannot but attract us, because it is, in one
way, the *extreme boundary* between what one is already
aware of, and what is still in process of formation.
Not only do you see there things that you experience
nowhere else, but one also sees emerge from within
one an underlying stream of clarity, energy, and freedom
that is to be found hardly anywhere else in ordinary life ...
and the new form that the soul then takes on
is that of the individual living the quasi-collective life of
all men, fulfilling a function far higher than that of
the individual, and becoming conscious of this new state.

—Pierre Teilhard de Chardin, *The Making of a Mind*

A GENTLE BREEZE LIFTED the periwinkle sheers that framed the window seat in the spacious bedroom where I peacefully and privately meditated, read, wrote, and mused.

On one end of the window seat, I built a small altar to Teilhard, the Jesuit mystic who had become my guide, companion, and ally. I propped the picture of Teilhard on the cover of Ursula King's *Spirit of Fire* against a small pile of books, lit a votive candle, and placed it next to a small vase of daises I picked in my yard. Everything was arranged in a tidy group of three.

I was writing my dissertation on the evolution of newspapers and the emergence of online news, and the window seat was the perfect shelf to hold the mounds of books, papers, notes, transcripts, and cassette tapes that I carefully collected as a doctoral student. I was keenly aware that these neat piles of research held the key to my future: a tenure-track teaching job and a good life for me and my sons.

I sat cross-legged on the beige carpeting and leaned against the double bed I bought when I moved out of the house where my children grew up. It was the only new thing in the rented condo; everything else was bought used or was passed down from a family member or friend. In fact, much of the condo's sparse but tasteful furnishings came from my parents' home in New Jersey. After they died within months of each other, I rented a conversion van and made the round trip from upstate New York to northern New Jersey in one day to save money.

Always saving money.

My mantra had become, "How much does it cost?" Too much was the frequent answer.

I glanced once more at the patrician nose and pursed lips of Teilhard on King's cover and closed my eyes to settle into meditation. My breath came easily as the tension in my body left in gentle waves.

Comforting bliss.

"Ruff."

I heard it again. Louder.

"Ruff."

It was Benny, Mike's dog, announcing that he needed to go out. Benny wasn't a barker like the Shih Tzus next door, who, once disturbed, barked incessantly. No, Benny usually barked once—or like today, twice to announce his need.

He was a good dog and a most excellent friend.

I rose from the impromptu altar to take him around the usual loop of the cul-de-sac. Walking Benny several times a day was the perfect punctuation for my writing and research, a necessary but silent interruption where I was free to keep on thinking but was also able to move my body.

A welcome quiet greeted me as I walked through the cozy neighborhood where I now lived. It was less than ten miles away from the marital residence, but it felt like a parallel universe where I was able to be with myself, my thoughts, my pain, and of course, to do my work.

I was studying how the nearby Albany *Times Union* began their shift from print to digital production, making it possible to publish their very first stories on their website. The biggest challenge *Times Union* programmers faced was working with the newspaper's proprietary production system: It was simply not easy to share files across platforms. So they used their expertise in exporting information to their library and archives to modify an existing program and get stories onto the web.

"It was a kluge of a kluge," the newspaper's IT guy gleefully told me about the process. This inelegant but expedient solution was the evidence I needed to prove my theory that media evolve.

Everything I read, understood, and felt inside told me it was possible to identify the moment when something never seen before appeared. Sure, there were incremental changes and choices made along the way, but it was ultimately a creative programming patch that connected the newspaper's library, where all their stories were stored, to the *Times Union*'s fledgling website.

Those lines of code made the entire enterprise work: The newspaper could now seamlessly move stories through their internal computer network and simultaneously publish them in print and on the web. Brilliant. Hidden away in the intricate language that programmers use to make computers work the way humans intend, there it was—a new and novel way of doing something that had never been done before.

I saw it as a first step in the emergence of a new medium.

I felt a new burst of power within myself, too. I was beginning to internalize the understanding that what was happening in my day-to-day reality started inside me somewhere: I was beginning to see, as Teilhard wrote, that I was indeed "the *center of construction*" of my universe.

More importantly, I was learning to control my thoughts and intentions. Writing my dissertation was hard, but I'd reached a point where I knew I was going to finish. I just didn't know when. I needed to find a job, too, but for now I calmly and methodically moved down my to-do list.

If Teilhard was right and "the entire fraction of the cosmos" is "open to our experience," it was me and only me that created the realities that showed up in my life. That required a deep and profound personal responsibility, not only for my actions but for my thoughts, beliefs, and attitudes, too.

The chaos of my life honed my perspective. Sitting in the living room reading from a long list of books to prepare for my candidacy exams disciplined me. I could sit, try to study, and get distracted by the pain of betrayal, or I could focus my attention on passing my candidacy exams.

I chose the latter and it served me well. Thank you, Teilhard.

I didn't know it at the time, but looking back, this was one of the best times of my life. I made definitive, clear choices, and I learned how to focus my energy on what was important to me: finishing my dissertation and getting a job. "What good is a PhD if you don't have a job?" one of my professors demanded.

My Rensselaer mentor suggested I find and wear the best clothing I could afford on job interviews, which was a challenge for a graduate student living on a stipend of twelve thousand dollars, a small maintenance from the pending divorce, and some financial help from my beloved Aunt Cor.

My college roommate and dear friend Lynda took me shopping at Stein Mart, a discount store with designer clothing, where I found a pink cashmere blazer for a fair price. Along with a black skirt I had from another shopping trip together—a splurge when money wasn't so tight—I was building an interview wardrobe.

I also shopped in consignment stores and spotted a beautiful charcoal gray suit that had been in a trunk show in New York City. I stood holding the hanger for a long time, staring but not ready to buy. It proved to be a useful strategy: The longer I remained undecided, the cheaper the suit became as the shop owner studied my face and lowered the price.

At seventy-five dollars, I bought it, knowing it would have to be altered. I could not wear a long skirt that looked like a tulip on the bottom. Once the "petals" were gone, it would still be long enough to appear sensible with the right shoes.

I took the suit to my favorite seamstress in downtown Troy on Fourth Street. She was from central Europe, and I think we were sisters in another life. She balked when I told her to remove the tulip petals, but she agreed. With a crisp white shirt, dark black hose, and loafers, it became my East Coast interview suit.

Like breadcrumbs left along a trail, I sensed these clothing adventures were subtle assurances that I was on the right track and could trust that I would get help when I needed it.

I began to see these flow moments as more than luck or coincidence: There was a sometimes strong, sometimes gentle force guiding me to the new life I coveted. "And if we are to be happy—completely happy ... We must add one stitch, no matter how small it be, to the magnificent tapestry of life;" Teilhard wrote in my favorite little volume, *On Happiness*, a series of sermons he delivered at the weddings of his family members. As I stayed sober, showed up in the lives of my children, avoided creating any more emotional wreckage, and discovered new ways to look at news, I was adding that "stitch" that Teilhard saw as essential to happiness.

In fact, I often felt like I wasn't just adding a stitch—I was sewing a whole patch.

I was beginning to see that each of my actions was sacred.

My whole life. All of it. Not just the fearful moments lying in bed at night, head spinning, staring at the ceiling, anxiety filling my dreams. Or the angry moments sitting in front of the computer writing, rewriting, and finally removing contemptuous emails to my not-quite-ex-husband.

All of it. The easy joy of watching my son Brendan play lacrosse, his long stick shimmering in the sun as he ran across the grass field on a perfect spring day. Sitting in the stands while Mike played hockey, feeding Benny soft ice cream, or meeting with my dissertation adviser.

All of it.

I was responsible for it all: the consequences of my actions and my inactions. In living this new way, I was creating my own reality. I started a daily meditation practice to slow my mind down, joined a twenty-four-hour gym to burn off my angst, and cooked comfort food for my sons and their friends.

I embraced Teilhard's "ever more perfect eyes" and stopped fighting what was. I put down the mantle of victimhood and picked up the sword of the victor. I stopped accusing outside forces, especially people, for creating the chaos and pain in my life.

Placing blame outside myself had become a comfortable pattern that kept me from looking at my own limitations and responsibility. I had drunk away, rationalized, and otherwise off-loaded my pain so I wouldn't have to face the only one that was accountable: me.

That one interior move changed everything.

If my whole life was a prayer, then everything, especially the pain, was an opportunity to transcend.

❧

I returned to the condo with Benny, ready to start working, opened the screen door, and smelled it.

Smoke.

I let Benny off his leash and ran through the living room, kitchen, and dining room. Nothing. I bounded up the stairs two at a time, ran into my bedroom, and saw bright orange, yellow, and blue flames licking the periwinkle sheers I'd hung so generously in front of the large window.

Within seconds the sheets disintegrated into black ash as my television, DVD player, and stereo melted into mounds before my eyes.

The intensity of the moment split me in two: My insides slowed down and my outsides sped up. There were two of me: one doing things, and one navigating what was about to happen.

In what may have been one of the most important decisions of my life, I decided not to run downstairs and retrieve the fire extinguisher from underneath the kitchen sink. Instead, I rushed to the bathroom, picked up the garbage can, emptied it on the floor, and filled it up with water from the bathtub faucet.

I looked at the window seat where my future lay in hopeful obedience: the books, papers, folders, notebooks, transcriptions, and cassette tapes sat in trusting piles, waiting to be saved. Years of work neatly organized, ready to yield my dissertation.

Flames. Water. Bathtub.
Flames. Water. Bathtub.
Flames. Water. Bathtub.

But the flames grew and it seemed I was losing the battle. The outside me picked up the phone and called the Halfmoon Fire Department. I quickly gave them my address, dropped the phone on the floor, and tuned in to the inside me.

Flames. Water. Bathtub
Flames. Water. Bathtub.
Flames. Water. Bathtub.

I did it.
I put it out.

I put out the fire.

Soot from the melted electronics covered the floor, walls, and everything in the room. I glanced over at the window seat where the mounds of books and papers that held my future silently rested. Intact.

I did it. I put out the fire.

I heard sirens, looked out the large bedroom window, and saw a small armada of fire trucks pull into the cul-de-sac.

My outsides screamed, "What took you so long? The firehouse is only a few miles away."

My insides rejoiced at the choice I made to stay and fight. To fight the fire alone. To protect my work, my future, my life.

I did it. I put out the fire.

I walked downstairs barefoot. Who knew what happened to my shoes? A fire marshal ordered me out of the house. I obliged. They led me, confused and dazed, to an ambulance where kindly EMTs bandaged my burned hand and unsuccessfully tried to take me to the hospital.

I now know I was in shock.

I did it. I put out the fire.

It took me more than twenty years to realize how different my life would have been if I hadn't put that fire out. What if my doctoral research had burned, as well as everything else in my bedroom, my condo, and perhaps the one next door, too? Would I have had the motivation to start over? I'll gratefully never know.

Where did my energy come from? Was it Teilhard's spirit running wild? Was the power so much bigger than me that I wasn't able to contain it?

Or did I save myself?

The first person I called afterward was Brendan. He was twenty then and working at a restaurant in nearby Saratoga Springs. When he arrived, he put the phone back on its hook, took the melted electronics out of my bedroom, walked Ben, and made me eat.

I sat on my bed in the soot-covered bedroom and watched while my son took care of me. I remembered the three-year-old dressed in a skeleton costume holding my hand on the way to a Halloween party; the same little guy with black smudges under his eyes who looked up and said, "I'm going to be shy," was all grown up.

When Brendan left for work, I called my friend Liz, who insisted on leaving work to drive me to the bank to deposit my rent check. A nurse friend came to my rescue, too. She had me soak my burned right hand in a bucket of ice water, and after her many kind requests, I agreed to take a bath.

When the bathwater darkened around me, I realized that my face, hair, and body were covered with a layer of the same black soot that stained my walls, ceiling, rugs, and furniture. As I rested my head against the back of the tub and let the warm water soothe me, the separation of self I experienced, the unbraiding of time, was resolved. I was gently and slowly woven back together.

And I went on with my life.

I became Dr. Christine M. Tracy; I wrote an ethnographic study of the development of the Albany *Times Union*'s website; I proved that media do evolve.

I was evolving too.

Five

What paralyzes life is lack of faith and lack of courage. The difficulty lies not in solving problems but expressing them correctly; and we can now see that it is biologically undeniable that unless we harness passion to the service of spirit there can be no progress. Sooner or later, then, and in spite of all our incredulity, the world will take this step—because the greater truth always prevails and the greater good emerges in the end.

—Pierre Teilhard de Chardin, *On Love & Happiness*

Las Vegas is an unlikely place for academics to meet, but the airfares were cheap, so that was the city the Rhetoric Society of America chose for its 2002 semiannual meeting. I was traveling to the conference to present a paper on the digital conversion of Leonardo da Vinci's Codex Leicester. I was intrigued by Bill Gates's decision to buy the precious notebook, take it apart, and digitize it. That is the joy of being a graduate student: I could indulge my curiosity.

A copy of Teilhard's *The Human Phenomenon* sat next to me on the seat—my traveling companion on this vacation from my demanding life. Reading his work felt like a luxurious indulgence when I had long lists of required reading. I was struggling my way through Teilhard's major works and had not yet discovered his letters and the gift of their accessibility.

The rich and sensuous scent of bergamot filled the cabin as the stewardess moved up the aisle offering beverages. She was wearing Shalimar perfume, which reminded me of a high school boyfriend, who gave it to me as a Christmas gift.

"Diet Coke, please," I said as I smiled at her.

My ticket was upgraded to the first-class cabin; it was a sign from the universe that I was being held, supported, and beloved amid so much inner and outer turmoil. I was in the third year of the doctoral program, preparing for my candidacy exams, about eight months sober, and not quite divorced.

I pressed the button that reclined the seat, rested my head on the headrest, and celebrated the small luxuries of the first-class cabin—more space, cushy upholstery, and almost-real food.

"From the flight deck, this is your captain. We'll be flying at thirty-five thousand feet. The sky is clear and there is a bit of a tailwind, so I expect we will land in Las Vegas a few minutes early. I'll be pointing out some sights along the way like the Grand Canyon, which will be visible on the left side of the cabin. Relax and enjoy the flight."

And I did.

Viewing the world from an elevated perspective, suspended in time and place, helped me see more clearly. It was a preview of one of the perks of my future life as a college professor, which included presenting papers at national and international conferences. I looked forward to visiting exciting cities—San Francisco, Berlin, and London.

One of the best parts of the trip was a long car ride into the Utah desert with my graduate school friends. As we drove through the curving blacktop of the desert on our way to the Hoover Dam, I felt carefree and even a little wild, like the heroines in *Thelma and Louise*.

We stopped for snacks at a small bodega—orange soda, chips, peanut butter crackers. The snaking road outside looked like something from a car commercial, and the burden of my imploding personal life felt very far away. I stopped imagining my husband of twenty-some years with his paramour, stopped seeing the two of them together on a clandestine rendezvous. I simply stopped ruminating and enjoyed being with my friends.

The unforgettable stench of the park service restroom—old urine cooked to a sweltering 110 degrees—made me forget about my problems, too. The relief from peeing was only briefly canceled out by the oppressive stench.

"What are you going to say to him?" a friend asked. This grand human endeavor in Utah was a fitting backdrop for a discussion of the disintegration of my marriage.

We stood and gazed at the Hoover Dam and contemplated the man-hours that went into creating one of humankind's most massive masonry since the Great Pyramids.

One of my classmates had been researching the history of the dam and recited some startling statistics: More than a hundred lives were lost building the dam that forever changed the natural course of the Colorado River. She was considering writing her dissertation on the dam's construction, but was concerned about devoting years to studying its dark past.

"My lawyer told me not to contact her or her husband. She thinks he may know already," I said in response to my friend's question.

"I still think you should tell him," she insisted. "Don't you think he has a right to know?"

I had thought about this. It made a lot of sense. Actually, it had a touch of altruism to it.

My husband's constant denials made me crazy. I know now I was being gaslit, something that can happen even to someone who is smart enough to win a full scholarship to a prestigious institution like Rensselaer.

I thought about telling her husband quite often, but I ultimately never did. Traveling, being with my friends, sitting by the pool at the hotel along the Las Vegas strip, soaking in the sun, and resting my weary soul was enough.

I decided to stay an extra day to work on my tan and my courage before I flew back to upstate New York and my tumultuous life.

My hotel was better than I had imagined. It had three pools of differing temperatures. My favorite was the slightly warm one. I walked over to its edge and slowly entered the light blue water. It was just cool enough to cancel the dessert heat, and I dipped down to cover my shoulders. I put my arms over my head and plunged into the water, floated on my back, and let the cool water absolve me of my sins, his sins, the sins of the world. More than anything, I appreciated the quiet and the absence of responsibility. No one asking me for anything. Nowhere to drive anyone. No dinners to make. No clothes to wash. No chapters to read, papers to write or grade. I sat at the side of the pool and simply felt the sun on my shoulders.

There were several good questions following my presentation on the digitization of Leonardo's notebook, which was always a sign that I was on the right track intellectually. There was only one thing left to do before I returned to New York State: practice for my candidacy exams with my dissertation chair, Professor Halloran.

I agreed to meet him in his suite the morning of the last day of the conference. He had a garden apartment like mine, but with a living room and kitchen area. The sun shone through the large skylight, and I was much calmer being away from the Troy campus to rehearse what I believed was the hardest part of the doctoral program.

The candidacy exam involved getting a "clean" laptop and answering three questions members of my committee submitted, with only a bibliography for reference. The prospectus, course work, and dissertation writing felt more predictable. I knew if I put in the time, I would see the result. But having a limited amount of time to answer questions on the fly after a year of reading felt much more daunting.

I was scared, which I knew was the kiss of death to clear thinking. I stared at the furniture in the room like a life-support system. Could the chairs be my allies?

I focused on the present, on the here and now, and not on the gruesome thoughts: I might not finish. I could fail my candidacy exams. Not get to finish my dissertation. Be asked to leave the program.

Finishing. Getting the degree. Graduating. Getting a job was my life raft to a promising future for me and my sons.

I felt so little sometimes. Not big enough for this endeavor.

I pulled at the hem of my green khaki skirt and admonished myself for not wearing something that covered my legs better when I sat down.

But it was hot; the forecast predicted one hundred degrees. Air conditioning everywhere. I could hear it humming silently in the background as my dissertation chair made us coffee. Ever the gracious human.

Professor Halloran returned with the drinks and started the questioning. It all went well—this was practice, after all—until he asked: "Why are you hesitating?"

"I'm hesitating because I'm trying to decide whether I'll tell you what I think you want to hear, or what I really believe," I said honestly.

Honesty. Such a novel concept. But I did truly believe one could not stay sober without it. I had about eight months then and didn't want to give up the hard-earned benefits of a clear mind and heart.

"If you don't tell me what you really think, you're going to fail," my chair said in his characteristically warm but firm diction.

We were discussing the invention of the internet, and I was reluctant to tell him that I believed it illustrated Teilhard's noosphere: the layer of thought energy that connects humanity. I didn't think there was a place for Teilhard's mysticism at Rensselaer, a technological university filled with computer scientists, engineers, and architects. I was discouraged from citing the work of the popular media theorist Marshall McLuhan, and was apprehensive about building a theoretical argument citing Teilhard.

His ideas had yet to be proven scientifically, and I was hesitant to use his work in my dissertation, concerned I might not get the approval of my committee. I later learned that exploring and documenting the profound interconnectedness of the universe fell to the Apollo 14 astronaut Edgar Mitchell, who had a deeply spiritual experience when he viewed the earth from space. Mitchell founded the Institute of Noetic Sciences to validate what Teilhard knew: We are all connected.

Just then something wild and crazy I still don't understand happened to my heart and my head. It felt like an invisible thread was weaving them together, forever and ever, amen.

YEAH! My heart and my head didn't need to be separate anymore.

Professor Halloran was asking for the truth. My truth. This brilliant and kind someone wanted to know what I really thought—not what I had practiced doing my whole life, telling people what they wanted to hear instead of what I really thought. The truth, my truth. He really wanted to hear my honest and true thoughts.

I sucked in my breath and launched into my understanding of Teilhard's noosphere and the web of invisible connections that led to the global network that became the internet.

"What we're now seeing—this weaving together and building of a network of ideas, words, and thoughts that began with Sir Tim Berners-Lee's hypertext markup language and evolved into the growing internet—is a demonstration of Teilhard de Chardin's noosphere: the sphere above the earth that collects human thought. It's something he saw, predicted, prophesied almost a hundred years ago. It's coming true.

"Thoughts are connected, or we wouldn't have an internet," I said finally. "It wouldn't exist."

Professor Halloran got up from his chair, walked around the small living room in the suite, and touched his beard a couple of times. I was familiar with these gestures from the many hours I spent in his classes.

"Teilhard offers a telos worthy of study," he said.

"Can you explain what telos means?" I asked. "Is it like logos, pathos, ethos?"

He answered the question by taking a small piece of paper from the pad on the desk at the hotel and writing: "Teilhard offers a telos worthy of study."

Telos. A cosmology.

In that moment, Professor Halloran, my trusted adviser, made it safe for me to show a part of myself that I'd kept hidden for fear of being dismissed, criticized, and judged as incompetent. He was also encouraging me to bring Teilhard into my academic research, which I had not yet felt safe or confident enough to do. Before this blessing, my study and exploration of Teilhard's writing, life, and ideas felt like a stealth enterprise, an unrequited passion that I jealously guarded. I could see the connection between his ideas about evolution and the transformation of communication technology I was witnessing, but until then, I hadn't had the courage to use Teilhard's writing and ideas in my work, which relied on rhetoric, hypertext theory, and a variety of media theorists to construct a prescient and credible argument.

"... Truth has to appear only once, in one single mind, for it to be impossible for anything ever to prevent it from spreading universally and setting everything ablaze," wrote Teilhard in the concluding line of "The Christic" in *The Heart of Matter*, written just before his death in 1955.

In the summer of 1925, powerful battles over the truth about evolution were being fought in the United States and across the globe in Paris, France.

In Dayton, Tennessee, the modernists' understanding that evolution could be consistent with religious beliefs faced off against the fundamentalist view that the word of God as revealed in the Bible took priority over human knowledge. The case became known as the Scopes Monkey Trial, with the famous politician and anti-evolutionist William Jennings Bryan facing off against Clarence Darrow, America's top criminal lawyer at the time. In a dramatic clash of modern and traditional values, the trial was broadcast throughout the United States and brought scientific evidence supporting evolution into the public sphere.

That same summer in Paris, Roman Catholic Church hierarchy ordered Teilhard to repudiate his progressive ideas explaining church dogma in light of modern evolutionary theory. His 1922 essay, "Note on Some Possible Historical Representations of Original Sin" challenged key tenets of the Catholic faith and was met with swift and powerful opposition.

His superiors ordered Teilhard to sign "The Six Propositions," a rigidly conservative document on original sin and human origin, to stop circulation of his theological writings, and, perhaps the most difficult, to leave his homeland, France, and his teaching position at the Institut Catholique de Paris.

The following spring, Teilhard stood on the deck of a steamer headed for Tianjin, China, where he would spend more than twenty years in what his biographers call a "self-exile."

Teilhard was banished from his homeland and forbidden to publish his work because he believed in the ongoing evolution of our individual souls and the world's soul—and the Catholic church did not.

Despite the banishment and his organic longing for France, his homeland, Teilhard let his internal compass guide him. His life in China was productive, full, and even celebrated. His reputation as an accomplished geologist and paleontologist grew. And as is the way of providence, while in exile in China, Teilhard was part of a research team that made one of the most important archaeological discoveries of all time: the bones of the Peking Man, an integral piece of evidence for Darwin's theory of evolution.

The Chinese had a special name for the tall, lanky Frenchman: De Ri Jin, which means "morality, sun, progress," and translates as "Father Daybreak Virtue." His internal light shone brightly despite the deep, personal heartache he suffered between 1932 and 1936 when his father, mother, brother Victor, and sister Guiguite all died during his absence.

Truth prevailed.

Professor Halloran's encouragement emboldened me to express my ideas about the power of the unseen becoming visible: I had witnessed the evolution of new communication technologies that could bring people all over the world together in unprecedented ways.

My truth prevailed, too.

Six

The day will come when, after mastering the ether, the winds, the tides, gravity, we shall master the energies of love, for God. And then, for the second time in the history of the world, man will have made fire his servant.

—Pierre Teilhard de Chardin, *The Evolution of Chastity*

"COME ON. WE'LL HAVE FUN," Nicole said.

"I have work to do," I said. I was afraid if I walked away from the mountains of tasks before me, I might never return.

"You always have a lot to do. It will be good for you to have a break. Liz is going, too," she said.

It took Nicole several phone calls before I finally agreed to fly to Providence on that overcast day in November 2002.

Our pilot was Nicole's husband Wally, who was studying at Rensselaer and working to get his pilot's license. I was sometimes invited to take short trips and help pay for the cost of renting a plane. I knew it would feel good to get out of Albany and especially to see the world from an elevated perspective.

"Okay, I'll go," I said.

Nicole, Liz, and Wally were good friends, and I always felt lighter and happier when I was with them.

"Why Providence?" I asked.

"Oh, there's a piece of art I want to see," Nicole answered quickly. "It's just the right distance from the Schenectady airport, too. We'll pick you up at 7:30 a.m.," she said.

Twenty-four hours later I was wandering around the Rhode Island School of Design (RISD) Museum in Providence.

I knew the campus and the city well because my sister went to Providence College and later RISD as a print-making major. I spent several weeks there helping her recover from a tragic Christmastime dorm fire in 1976.

The RISD Museum has a maze-like structure, and I soon found myself the solitary visitor on a winding staircase.

Alone was good and felt familiar.

"Dissertating" does that to you.

I climbed to the top and entered a small gallery filled

with silver. As I wandered through the quiet and peaceful rooms, my thoughts quickly went, as they constantly did, to my unfinished doctoral dissertation.

When I was working, it was intense, grueling, and consuming: I longed for the sense of completion that still eluded me, so I never felt peaceful or at ease.

A fragment of one of Teilhard's prayers came into my head as I stared at the large oil paintings: "We are quite naturally impatient in everything to reach the end without delay. We should like to skip the intermediate stages."

I longed to bypass the hard parts—the diligence, discipline, and sustained focus required to write a doctoral dissertation and earn a PhD. I needed "grace and circumstance," as Teilhard wrote, to guide me.

Yes, I nodded my head. Trust in the slowly, deliberately moving universe. I signed up for this. This was a critical piece of my growth: I must see it through to the end.

I turned a corner and was simultaneously surprised, elated, and speechless. One whole wall of the gallery was filled with a large and luminous oil painting: Frank Benson's *Summer*, a work that filled me with awe and wonder.

It took a few moments to take it in—not just because I was seeing the original for the first time after years of admiring reproductions on the walls of doctors' and dentists' offices—but also because I was recognizing the glorious and loving surprise gift from my dear friends.

I stood and stared.

But mostly I just felt.

Everything made sense now: the flight to Providence to give me a gift I did not realize I longed for—the opportunity to stand in front of Benson's oil painting in the RISD Museum.

My heart was overflowing. Liz had been tracking my wanderings in the museum and secretly gathered Wally and Nicole to join me in the revelatory moment.

I looked at them and saw tears filling their eyes.

"Oh," was all I said.

One of Benson's many gifts is his ability to capture light, and he uses white and gold paint with such grace and subtlety that the image literally shimmers. It is simply breathtaking to stand before it.

I stood staring at the dramatic painting and closely listened as a nearby docent described it to a small group of museum visitors.

Benson had three daughters: Eleanor, Elizabeth, and Sylvia. In *Summer*, Benson focuses on his daughter

Eleanor, who stands on the cliffs of the rocky Maine shore shielding her eyes against the sun. She towers above her sisters, who sit peacefully at her feet and gaze up at her in admiration and affection. Her energy fills the canvas, and her glimmering body radiates confidence, courage, and power.

Benson paints the sisters wearing long, flowing white linen dresses with long puffed sleeves and high necks carefully cinched at the waist with satin ribbons. He successfully captured the romance of the Gibson Girl, an image created by the artist Charles Dana Gibson in his pen and ink drawings of the late nineteenth and early twentieth centuries.

Gibson combined older images of American female beauty—the voluptuous woman and fragile lady—into a new portrayal of feminine beauty. With their slender curves, tiny waists, and bouffant hair, Gibson Girls radiated contentment, confidence, and ease.

In sharp contrast, I was wearing jeans with a sweater, T-shirt, and sturdy, practical shoes—very much the forty-something mother and graduate student living in upstate New York dressed to ride in a small, cold airplane. I longed to possess the contentment of the Benson sisters, especially Eleanor, who projected feminine power and wisdom as she towered above her sisters seated below.

We looked very different on the outside, but on the inside, I believed Eleanor and I were alike. Like Eleanor, I had needed to shield my eyes, not from the sun, but from the unpredictability of the future.

Nicole, Liz, and Wally understood my soul's connection to this great painting. They saw something in me that I could not yet see in myself: the courage, strength, and wisdom I demonstrated and possessed. Their love and support encouraged the fledging spirit inside me to soar a little higher.

Nicole was the first to speak. "It's like an Oprah moment," she said softly. It was her idea to bring me here, and she was pleased.

She knew too much talk would spoil the intention, the connection she created, the profoundness of the gift she facilitated, so she graciously offered me silence.

I traveled hundreds of miles in a small, noisy airplane to be here. Be now. It was an opportunity to practice presence, to be wrapped in love. And it became much more. Later, I returned to this memory again and again to see and hold what I now know is my higher self. To bring her to the moment, any moment, with joy and ease.

I stored that feeling in my body. Celebrated the knowing and came to rely on it in times of crisis, confusion, and pain.

So, this is what love feels like. The real thing. Knowing I was connected changed everything.

Seven

What would we do without our enemies?...
Exterior emergencies or shocks are indispensable to
force individuals out of their natural laziness
and set routines—and also to periodically break the
collective frameworks that imprison them.

—Pierre Teilhard de Chardin, *The Human Phenomenon*

WHEN I FIRST STEPPED onto the St. Anselm College campus, it was so quintessentially beautiful that I imagined I was in heaven. The campus sits atop a hill overlooking the picturesque city of Manchester. Clusters of wise trees and manicured walkways surrounding its Gothic buildings reminded me of my alma mater, Villanova University.

It was early 2005, I had just turned fifty, and I'd entered the highly competitive tenure-track job market. St. Anslem was my fifth on-campus interview.

As I stood next to my faculty host and gazed down at the city of Manchester from an elevated perspective, I imagined myself living there, teaching there, starting my new life there. I wondered what Mike would think. Would he be happy? He was in his junior year of high school, and I was painfully aware that starting his senior year in a new school and a new state would be difficult.

He watched me prepare for interviews in California, Michigan, Philadelphia, and now New Hampshire. In a stunningly gracious act for a seventeen-year-old, he generously said: "Mom, you worked hard. I watched you. You should take the best job you can get."

Mike recently got his braces off and had handsomely grown into his tall body. He played ice hockey in a small local league in Troy, and I pictured him joining Manchester teams and playing lacrosse in the spring, too.

I closed my eyes, looked up at the sky and saw Brendan joining us in Manchester for ski and snowboarding trips to the nearby White Mountains. We'd have relaxed and cozy Christmas dinners, and in the summer my sons would swim or surf in the nearby Atlantic Ocean.

It wouldn't be easy for him, but I was confident that Mike's sophistication, sense of humor, and social skills would help him easily adjust to living in a new state. He was also keenly aware of the financial necessity of a move for our family, and I was grateful for his support.

As I toured the campus, the oak-filled rooms literally shimmered in the low winter sunlight. After two decades in upstate New York, I had made friends with cold weather: the crunch of the snow, the crispness of the air, and the jolt that greets you when you step outside.

The English Department faculty corridor looked as if from a scene in a movie: creamy, almost golden oak doors, sun pouring in from the beveled windowpanes that opened to a nearby forest, the requisite bookcases, large wooden desks, and accompanying green leather chairs.

When I closed my eyes, I saw myself in one of the offices with my name, Dr. Christine M. Tracy, on the door. As I walked down the hall and turned the key in the door, all would be waiting for me—my books, my pictures, my diploma hung on the wall. I saw myself at my desk talking wisely to a young undergraduate sitting across from me in a small wooden chair.

"You have to write your way into the thinking, not think your way into the writing," I would say in response to the confusion that plagued all writers, especially young ones. I would expound on these and the other kernels of wisdom I'd gleaned from teaching writing for almost a decade.

My campus host, Professor J., was a spry woman in her middle forties. She talked easily, excitedly, and knowledgeably about my research and was impressed with my theoretical understanding of hypertext theory, which is the backbone of the internet's linking structure. I was flattered, grateful, and temporarily at ease during the long day of interviews. I knew my theoretical knowledge, technical understanding of the still burgeoning internet, and reporting experience ably qualified me for the job, but I also needed to be a good fit with the department to get an offer.

I had heard from several friends and colleagues that St. Anslem, nationally known for its political debates, wanted a Rensselaer graduate to round out its faculty. Knowing this gave me a bit more confidence as I prepared for the "money talk" with the head of the English Department.

The campus was lovely, and I breathed into the place within that felt the rightness of my professorial adventure. Deep down, in that lasting place of truth inside, I knew I was following the call of my soul. I had found a deep and profound peace during my many years as a student walking on Rensselaer's campus absorbing the quiet, stability, and dignity.

That peace comforted my nerves as I sat across from the department chair and talked money.

I stared patiently and attentively at his stern countenance as he told me the starting salary and then looked carefully at my face to gauge my reaction. The chair's number was significantly less than the offer I finally accepted, and lower than the already modest offer I had received from Russell Sage College where I worked for several years.

Looking back now, I imagine he needed to maintain an air of gravity to make the offer, which required teaching four sections of oral communication each semester.

"Is there room for negotiation?" I asked.

"No. That is the amount we are able to offer an assistant professor," he stoically replied.

The more I interviewed, the more comfortable I became with answering hard questions as well as not reacting to surprising information, such as the low salary. I was on my own now: no husband, two sons to guide and help support, a new life to design and build. I made a mental note about my financial pressures and again considered the offer I had from the college in Troy, where I was teaching part-time.

I was calm and composed because I knew deep down that I would make a good choice, which could be as simple as taking the next step on the path unfolding before me. I took great comfort, too, from the wise and practical counsel I received from my Rensselaer professors, who offered both scholarly and logistical advice as I navigated the demanding doctoral program.

Not long after I celebrated the completion of my dissertation at a weekend yoga retreat, I got a call from my faculty adviser:

"Have you applied anywhere?" he asked.

"I'm going to do a limited job search in the Philadelphia area. I want to work at St. Joe's, a Jesuit school," I said.

"That's not the best job out there," he declared. "What good is a PhD if you don't have a job? You don't know where you want to be. Apply everywhere," he insisted as he explained the fortuitous turn his own life took when he accepted a job at a big university on the East Coast.

I held this wisdom inside as I responded to the chair's salary offer with a slight nod and dutifully asked about annual raises and increases for tenure and promotion. But no matter how I looked at it, it was simply a lot of work for not a lot of money.

On most campus visits, I moved through an itinerary that included the campus and city tour, meeting students, teaching a class, individual meetings with faculty and administrators, and, the hardest part, the collective grilling by the department faculty. The scrutiny was excessive, but given the longevity of professors in university departments, it was understandable.

I told myself the only way I could mess up the interview was to be nervous. That was the mantra I repeated as I got ready to be interrogated: *Don't be nervous. Don't be nervous. Don't be nervous.*

On each of the campuses I visited, I realized the faculty were searching for the candidate they believed would best help them move their scholarly mission forward and who would also fit well within often eclectic departments.

I stepped into a conference room in one of the stone buildings on campus, stared at the long wooden table where I would soon present my research, and was overcome by fear.

The stakes were high. I needed a job, preferably a good, well-paying one located in a beautiful place. While the salary was quite low, the attractiveness of the campus on that crisp February day felt like additional compensation.

"Can I use the restroom?" I asked Professor J. I needed a few minutes alone to build my confidence.

"Sure. It's right this way. You have five minutes before we start," she said, pointing to the long table surrounded by a dozen chairs that would soon be filled by faculty members.

As I walked to the ladies' room, I could see the conference room filling up. Fear felt like vomit rising from my stomach to my throat and mouth. And I couldn't push it down with my brain—outthink it, outrun it, outsmart it.

When I closed the door to the ladies' room, a battle erupted between my longing and my angst: *I deserve to be here. I worked so hard. I am now following the breadcrumbs that brought me to this moment. Relax. I will be great.*

But I am nervous, scared, and certainly not worthy of all the shiny, warm wood in this place. I am not smart enough for this job, even if the pay is appalling.

I had less than five minutes to overcome fear that felt like a crazy fog filling up my insides and blinding me.

I need a job. This is a very good place to start my academic career. Some of the faculty get me. The campus is beautiful. I can see my sons living here. I would find a cozy, three-bedroom house for us with a big family room. The boys would have space to invite friends to watch movies and play video games, and I would happily supply them with popcorn and pizza.

But the dream I held in my heart increased the pressure I felt inside.

"Don't be nervous. Don't be nervous. Don't be nervous," I recited aloud this time. I knew deep down all the wanting would prevent me from being my true self.

But somehow knowing that didn't work.

Help!! my lower-self cried. *I'm scared! Help me, please!!*

I knew I needed more than the force of my own will to squash my fear and anxiety. I stared at the wooden door of the stall and took a long, deep breath. I closed my eyes and imagined Teilhard during the height of the battle of Verdun, crawling under barbed wire with the dead body of his friend, Captain Courtiaux, on his back.

After his return to the trenches, he gazed back on the battlefield and wrote:

> ... you seem to feel that you're at the final boundary between what has already been achieved and what is striving to emerge. ... the mind, too gets something like an overall view of the whole forward march of the human mass, and feels not quite so lost in it. It's at such moments, above all, that one lives what I might call "cosmically"—aroused intellectually as much as emotionally ...

Teilhard called it living cosmically.

I call it my interior navigation.

I reached deep down inside and turned it on as I struggled to find a way to get rid of the fear rising inside of me. I closed my eyes and took myself to the moment I walked into the gallery at the RISD Museum and saw the Benson painting.

Help arrived from that place of holiness and light where miracles exist. It arrived as a memory of being loved.

I was loved. I knew it.

I closed my eyes and turned on my own "cosmic vision." I saw myself walking into the gallery, absorbing the energy of Eleanor in Frank Benson's *Summer*, swimming in the great love and affection of my friends who brought me that moment.

In my mind, I saw my friends crying. And I felt the energy of their love. It was real. Tangible. And could be called up upon request. I know because that's exactly what I did then. I closed my eyes and felt the memory of being beloved, joyful, transcendent.

My fear subsided.

I held that energy inside like an invisible blanket of comfort, and not only comfort, but joy too. I felt joyful, confident, courageous, and smart as I walked out of the ladies' room into the big conference room where the St. Anselm English Department faculty waited.

I sat down at the head of the table in front of my computer, where a carefully timed blue-and-yellow PowerPoint presentation patiently waited for me. I had used it at other interviews, and it felt like a kindly friend that I could depend on to stay focused and calm.

It was a bright day and yellow sunbeams danced across the room.

I smiled and nodded at each of the faculty members, whose chairs scraped along the floor and creaked as they sat down. It smelled like books, lemon oil, and an old furnace—the perfume of academia.

I sat down and felt my "team" close by my side—the progressive faculty who read the same literature I would soon be citing, who understood hypertext theory and the recent shifts in media literacy. They were my allies, and I felt their goodwill and support.

But that wasn't the case further down the table, where other alliances prevailed.

I realized then I had not met the department's medievalist, a scholar who typically studies Chaucer, Spencer, and the literature of the Middle Ages. I wondered if some of the daylong interviews were structured to keep us apart. And now here she sat, with hunched shoulders and what looked like a permanent scowl.

After everyone was seated, I launched into my presentation, moving easily from the history of American journalism to the present, focusing on the invention of the internet and its amazing backbone, hypertext markup language, otherwise known as HTML. Sir Tim Berners-Lee created HTML in 1989 while working at the CERN particle physics laboratory in Switzerland and gifted this miraculous means of sharing information which changed the world forever.

I proudly explained how I identified a moment when a new medium was born. While studying the Albany *Times Union*'s transition from print to digital form, I discovered that an ingenious programming patch made it possible to move stories from the library on the "print side" directly to their website, where stories were automatically published in real time. It may not sound like much now, but it was a miracle then.

I made a thoughtful, passionate, and perceptive argument for the future of news and the unfolding evolution of media and communication technology. I was about three-quarters of the way through my talk when the medievalist interrupted me.

"I don't know what you're talking about!" she declared in a loud voice from behind her dark-rimmed glasses and large circle of jet-black hair.

Her words hit me like a cold bucket of water. I was surprised by her almost violent dismissal of my ideas and confused about why she didn't politely ask for clarification earlier in my highly theoretical presentation.

I worked hard to regain my composure as I returned to tracing the history of hypertext back to its oral roots, but my momentum was gone. Her question felt like a blow to my midsection. It momentarily took my breath away, but I knew I had another option besides fear and self-doubt. There was now a place inside me I could go: Teilhard described it as an "underlying stream of energy and freedom." My internal compass was lit up by the memory of my friends' demonstration of their love. Like Teilhard on the battlefield, I shifted my focus inward and quickly recovered.

"Are you not clear about what hypertext theory is? Which concepts are you struggling to understand?" I asked the medievalist.

"I just don't understand why all this technology is so important," she said, shaking her head dismissively. "Just go on."

And that's exactly what I did: I opened my mouth and let my hard-earned knowledge and innovative ideas flow gracefully from my passion for my work.

"What would we do without our enemies?" Teilhard asked. He offered this eloquent answer: "Exterior emergencies or shocks are indispensable to force individuals out of their natural laziness and set routines—and also to periodically break the collective frameworks that imprison them."

Sometimes those "exterior emergencies or shocks" are literally just that—a hurricane, tsunami, or earthquake. More often, they are more subtle and personal—a job loss, profound betrayal, or a chronic illness. Teilhard believed in the natural order of all things, which means not only seeing their rightful place but welcoming these evolutionary challenges. It is how he lived his life: why his whole life was a prayer.

I didn't get the job at St. Anselm, and I now know it wasn't because of the medievalist. The oak-paneled, light-filled space that would have been my office and the beauty of the campus perched atop the city of Manchester were very attractive, but St. Anselm College and Manchester, New Hampshire weren't where I belonged. I was beginning to trust my gut, and I didn't regret not getting a job offer. I knew I had brought my "A game," as my sons liked to say when I was using my power to the fullest. That was, and is, enough.

Eight

I incline to believe that the source of most of our
weaknesses is to be found in the fact that we
do not "believe" to the very end, nor on a wide enough
scale: to stop believing a second too early,
or to believe in an inadequate object, can be enough
to ruin the whole edifice we are building.

—Pierre Teilhard de Chardin, *Letters to Leontine Zana*

"Where's Heidi?" I asked my son Mike on the Friday afternoon before my graduation ceremony.

It was May of 2005, and I was officially Christine M. Tracy, PhD. I had a tenure-track teaching position—the gold star—and no debt once I paid Rensselaer for a parking ticket.

I had accepted a position at Eastern Michigan University, a large public university in southeast Michigan, and bought a charming little house in Ann Arbor's historic district.

It was a big, brave move: I didn't know anyone in the state except my new colleagues, and our family would be far apart geographically. Mike was moving

with me, and Brendan would continue living with his father in upstate New York. I waited until the very last min-
ute to tell my beloved Aunt Cor about the move because
she would now be thousands of miles away instead of a
three-hour drive from upstate New York to New Jersey.

To help ease Mike's transition to a new state, new
friends, and a new school, I agreed to buy him expensive
ice hockey pads and to get a companion for our beloved
white-shepherd/lab mix of five years, Ben.

Mike is a "dog whisperer" of sorts. He was able to
see Ben's light when he was abandoned in the Saratoga
County Animal Shelter in Ballston Spa after his owner
went to jail.

Ben was in terrible shape when Mike decided to
adopt him. He was thin and scared with painful sores on
his body. In the years we were blessed to own him, Ben
returned that faith and courage over and over.

So I trusted Mike when we went from shelter to
shelter until we found Heidi. Her eyes were bright blue,
and she weighed forty pounds, about the same as Ben. In
a replay of his selection process, Mike looked at her and
decided she was the one.

After a visit to the local PetSmart for a bath, Heidi's true beauty was uncovered: She was a small red husky, and once she was washed, her bright blue eyes truly shone. Mike had worked his magic again.

But I couldn't find her in the house that afternoon.

"She was just here a second ago," Mike said.

I looked at the front door and saw the screen door ajar.

"Oh no! She got out!" I said.

Mike and I raced to our cars and began driving around the neighborhood. I stopped every cluster of people I saw and asked with growing desperation:

"Have you seen a little red husky? We live on Cobble Court, and she got away," I said.

As I slowly drove through the sprawling developments of Clifton Park, my anxiety grew. Why didn't I get her one of those metal tags with my phone number on it? My brother Blair was coming from New Jersey in a few hours with two of my aunts, Corinne and Betty. I hadn't finished getting their rooms ready and cleaning the house, or started dinner.

After an hour or more, Mike and I sadly gave up the search.

"I guess she's gone. Who knows where she is now," he said dejectedly.

"There's nothing we can do now but pray and see her finding her way back to us. I don't know how that's possible, Mike, but I believe it is."

Yes. Trust. Here was that t-word again. "We don't believe through to the end," wrote Teilhard. Well, this wasn't the end. The end would be Heidi's return.

I went back to my preparations. Pride and joy in my accomplishment replaced my anxiety about Heidi. I was Dr. Christine M. Tracy, forever and ever, amen.

The next day, I would walk across the stage and RPI President Dr. Shirley Ann Jackson would place the red and white doctoral hood over my shoulders. I did it. I was done. I never gave up when it became impossibly hard: when I moved out of the four-bedroom colonial where I raised my sons; when I carried a plastic milk carton filled with books, notes, and papers up to a friend's small cabin in the Adirondacks to work in quiet and solitude.

I never gave up when I struggled to keep visions of my husband's infidelity out of my brain. I instead filled it with rhetorical genre theory, hypertext theory, and the history of American journalism.

As a fitting reward for my years of hard work, my

graduation day on a Saturday in May dawned a bright and spectacular blue.

I was lost in thought as I drove the familiar route from my condo to the campus. I parked near the Rensselaer track, picked up the hanger from the back seat, and put on the big, heavy red velvet gown that told the world I was one of those "doctor people."

The sky was aqua, the trees were full of green swaying leaves, and all was right with the world. My heart was singing with joy. I did it. I jumped through all the hoops, passed all the tests, showed them I had the right stuff—over and over again, I ably met the challenges before me. I put my head down, focused on the task before me, asked the right people for help when I needed it, and now here I was—standing on the very spot on my university's campus where my college sweetheart and husband of twenty-something years chose to regularly meet his paramour.

In that moment, Teilhard's courageous spirit surrounded me like an intoxicating perfume. I held the pain of betrayal deep within me, and as Teilhard promised, I faced the challenges before me and walked forward with as much grace as possible.

Our biggest mistake, he wrote in *On Love and Happiness*, is that we give up before the end: "What paralyzes life is lack of faith and lack of courage. The difficulty lies not in solving problems but expressing them correctly."

I believed. I acted. I persevered.

And now here I was, fully present during one of the most glorious moments of my life.

With each paper I wrote, each book I read, each class I taught, and each hurdle of the doctoral program I surmounted, I was adding that "one stitch" to Teilhard's "magnificent tapestry of life."

The ceremony hadn't started yet, but my toes ached from the strappy, high-heeled black sandals I was wearing, a splurge because I knew they would be the only thing showing while I wore the red doctoral robe.

The sounds of Celtic bagpipe music filled the air and signaled the beginning of the ceremony.

"My feet hurt," I said to my friend Nicole, who caught my eye as I walked up the aisle, careful not to catch a high heel in the plastic flooring that covered the Rensselaer track.

"You look great!" she said.

"I love this robe," I said and lightly touched the velvet on my sleeve and the black cap with the tassel that was just a little too big for my head.

I sat down in a small white folding chair, looked for my family in the wheelchair section where my aunts were seated, waved, and settled in as the procession of graduates continued.

So much behind me.

So much ahead.

Is it necessary to drag oneself through life on one's belly, like a salamander crawling close to the ground, inhaling dirt? Never looking up. Focused on the next few inches ahead. Moving slowly, waiting for a harsh wind to whip up a blinding storm.

It was for me.

I needed every moment of heartache, pain, and mostly self-imposed chaos to bring me to this moment. As I looked up at the white clouds dotting the striking blue sky that May morning, I thought about the deep sense of betrayal Teilhard felt when he realized his essay "Note on Certain Historical Representations of Original Sin" had been stolen from his desk drawer at the Institut Catholique de Paris.

It was a heady time for Teilhard. He had returned from WWI as a decorated hero, finished his PhD at Sorbonne, held a prestigious teaching position, and was gaining celebrity in Europe as a progressive thinker for his insights on the unity of science and religion.

Then his life dramatically changed.

The forces of jealousy, hatred, and fear reared their ugly heads, and in one swoop, Teilhard's life was irrevocably altered. The world would have to wait until after his death to receive his teachings about the essential unity of all things in an evolving universe.

I shifted slightly to settle more comfortably in the chair I would be sitting in for several hours, smiled, and turned to the student sitting next to me, who wore a big, heavy red doctoral robe like mine.

"Is your family here today?" I asked.

"Yes. My parents came from DC and my wife is here with our infant son. She's probably lurking in the back, in case he cries," he said.

"Well, congratulations," I said.

"You, too. How long did it take you?" he asked.

"Five years. I spent the last year writing my dissertation," I said. He nodded, and we returned to our solitary thoughts.

I ran my fingers over the soft black velvet and touched the tassel on my hat that told the world I did it: I earned the three letters *PhD* after my name.

Five years.

So much had happened since 1999 when I started the program. I had been full of bravado, brazened by alcohol, and deluded about the state of my life and my marriage.

I know now that while finishing the degree is one of my life's greatest accomplishments, getting sober in 2001 has had just as much—if not more—impact on not only the quality of my life, but also its direction.

It didn't stick the first time I tried to stop drinking, more than fifteen years before earning my PhD, when I blacked out at my cousin's wedding. I was still moving around, walking, talking, and of course drinking, but my actions weren't registering in my brain. But it clicked when I told my sister, "I have to call and check on the boys," and she replied, "You just did that."

I didn't remember.

It scared me that I had two young children, and I was consuming so much alcohol that I blacked out.

After the blackout, I stopped drinking and stayed

stopped for almost ten years. But like a moving freight train, I picked up again when I thought I could drink safely. It took me more than ten years and several tries to begin the twenty-three years of continuous sobriety I have today.

I retreated from my musing when Hilary Clinton walked up to the microphone to give the commencement address. It was the spring of 2005 and a lot of her story had yet to unfold. At that time, she was a senator from New York and talked passionately about a recent trip to the Arctic Circle to encourage Rensselaer graduates to take up the cause of the earth. Her message perfectly suited the university's motto—"Why not change the world?"—which was featured in marketing materials and hung on a banner across Troy's Fifteenth Street footbridge.

As I watched the procession of graduates and felt waves of inner peace, I saw the paradox of this precious moment: The source of my deep sorrow was also the source of my great joy. "See or perish, this is the human condition," wrote Teilhard in *The Human Phenomenon*, and I understood what it meant to not run away from the truth.

I was seeing my life, especially the most painful and difficult challenges, more clearly and consciously. That clarity was greatly enhanced by the realization that I wasn't waging a battle: No one was against me; my life circumstances were a necessary part of my evolution.

Teilhard's conversion came on the battlefield in Verdun, when he felt the whole universe surging and ebbing, when the "boundary between what has already been achieved and what is striving to emerge" became clear and he embraced the understanding that he was connected to everything.

Evolution isn't just about the dinosaurs, a comet striking the earth, or humans descending from apes. We are individually and collectively the bearers of evolution. Once I understood this and began living this way, I was transformed.

When we got back to my condo after the graduation ceremony, there was a message on my answering machine.

"I think I have something that belongs to you," said the gentle and kind-hearted stranger who explained that our dog Heidi had stopped on his front porch to eat a box of Krispy Kreme donuts. The stranger reminisced about suffering as a young boy because his beloved dog ran away. Here was his chance to return a wayward pet to its owner.

Heidi came home to us, and I came home to myself.

Nine

Love is the most universal, the most tremendous
and the most mysterious of cosmic forces ....
Love is a sacred reserve of energy; it is like the
blood of spiritual evolution.

—Pierre Teilhard de Chardin, *Human Energy*

"LOOK, THERE'S THE SUN!" Michiganders shout when they see rays of light peeking from behind the winter cloak of clouds.

Mike and I were in a Whole Foods buying water and snacks for his soccer team on a gray Saturday in 2005. He was a senior at a private high school in Ann Arbor and was adjusting well to our big move to the Midwest. My sons were growing up. Brendan had just turned twenty-one, and was working and going to college in New York State.

I drove Mike to the soccer field and returned home to start the mountains of work that I faced as an assistant professor at Eastern Michigan University

(EMU), one of the state's fifteen large, public research universities. Founded in 1849 as a teacher's college, EMU is affordable, accessible, and diverse, with a welcoming environment for first generation students.

It was a good job with a very different culture than my experiences in classrooms on the East Coast. When I walked into my Introduction to Journalism class on my first day, forty freshman and sophomores sat in silence. I felt their eyes on me as I stood in front of the class and placed my books, files, and briefcase on the desk. Their silence was deafening, and I was unnerved by the sharp contrast between their reticence and the lively banter that greeted me when I walked into classes at Russell Sage College where I had worked for years.

My new home became a soft nest and safe haven to ease my transition. Mike had a ride home from the game, so I settled into the soft, brown leather chair in my cozy living room and took great comfort in my decision to buy this small cottage-style house in a charming residential area just a few blocks from downtown Ann Arbor. I loved living in my new neighborhood with its spacious white front porches, pea-gravel driveways, and postage-stamp backyards. The proximity to my neighbors made me feel safe and protected. It felt like a special reward for getting through the divorce, finishing the doctoral program, and completing the big move to the Midwest.

This was the first house I owned by myself, and I splurged on a piece of real art, a watercolor called *Eat Your Watermelon* by Michelle Tsosie Sisneros, an artist I met at the Indian Market in Santa Fe. As I sat down to work, I stared up at the three sisters, with their webbed feet, sucking juicy pieces of ripe watermelon.

"I need to paint the walls a different color," I mused as I stared at the yellow walls and considered the changes that I wanted to make to the house. I finally started focusing on my prep for my graduate class Writing in a Networked World, which was an opportunity to practice my new knowledge. The gentle wind pushed a branch of the scarlet red burning bush in front of the house against the windowpane, and the noise returned my attention to the rising pain in my chest. I had been successfully ignoring it for hours, but the persistent pressure made that impossible.

Like a boot on my chest, I felt a growing heaviness. My breath came in short, shallow bursts. Was this a sober panic attack or a real heart attack, like the one I had witnessed in someone I knew for a long time?

For the last six years, time had become my enemy. Never, never, ever enough time to do, do, do. Always, always, always so much to do as a mother, full-time student, teaching assistant, and human being: dinners, family birthdays, holidays, dentist appointments, teacher conferences, sleepovers, homework, and sports. Reading, class preps, grading, writing, conferences, meetings, revisions, and research.

There was always another technology to learn, job search to manage, resume to write, interview to plan, flight to book, and on and on. Somehow the years of constant overwhelm enveloped me on that oh-so-gray Saturday afternoon in Ann Arbor, where I sought comfort in the hundred-year-old house that was mine, all mine.

I tried the calming techniques my massage therapist recommended. I slowed my breath down and focused on the in-and-out, but the pain continued, and with it, rising fear. My thoughts spun out of control, and I felt alone and scared. My doctor friend R.'s advice echoed loudly in my head: "If you even think you're having a heart attack, go to the hospital. Don't wait! It's so much better to go and have them say, 'false alarm' than to not go."

What is a heart attack, really? Is it when the body's source of wisdom and power attacks it? Shuts it down? I now know the heart has a brain that is perhaps more intelligent than the one in our heads because it is so intimately connected to our emotions and our central nervous system. The warning signs, the pounding and tightening pain, are a loud, clear alarm to stop everything and pay attention.

What message was my heart sending me?

Had my power center turned on me?

I had watched a heart attack unfold before, and so on that fall afternoon in Ann Arbor, I clearly understood the dangers of a missed diagnosis.

The doer part of me—the one who regularly functioned on six hours of sleep, who gave up drinking, and who took a tenure-track job in a state where she only knew her new colleagues—watched my mind and body collapse into pain and fear. What is life, really, but a series of small miracles? Or is it a giving over to the truth? I now believe it is both. Facing life head-on and moving courageously through the pain taught me that life's lessons come in these moments of truth, which is quite miraculous.

I called another doctor friend, C., who was my new neighbor. "Go sit on your front porch," she said. "I will pick you up and drive you to the University of Michigan hospital. I can't go in with you because my son is with me, but I will tell you what to say so they see you right away: Tell them you think you're having a heart attack."

Within minutes, she pulled up in front of my house. "Get in," she insisted, and I reluctantly walked down the steps of my front porch, got in the backseat of her Volvo station wagon, and buckled my seat belt next to her five-year-old son who stared at me from his car seat.

She drove quickly to the nearby ER.

"I have chest pain and I think I'm having a heart attack," I repeated as a concerned nurse placed a blood pressure cuff on my right arm. The Velcro strip made that familiar "rupp" sound, and I was plugged into monitors and given my first dose of nitroglycerin.

I thought nitroglycerin was an explosive and wondered about its efficacy. I rested my head on the pillow and began to loosen my tight grip of resistance, relaxing into a graceful surrender. Teilhard was teaching me to trust, to be vulnerable when I felt like fighting. In his poetic essay and prayer "Mass on the World," he described the pain, suffering, and death of the battlefield of Verdun as a "baptism of reality."

Life calls us again and again to face what is real.

"Am I having a heart attack?" I asked the blue-clad doctor when she saw me about an hour later. "We'll know after we do the blood gasses," she said. I sat in silence. Waiting. Worrying. Fearing. Feeling my tight, cramped chest and shallow breathing.

In the University of Michigan Emergency Department, employees wore different color scrubs to help patients identify and distinguish their functions. Doctors and physician assistants: gray. Nurses: navy blue. Technicians: olive green. Clerks: burgundy. Registrars: beige. My fears escalated as I sat in my open-backed hospital gown, responded to the requests of the rainbow of beings moving around me, and listened to the constant beeping of the monitors.

No books, no television, no phone. I entertained myself by eavesdropping on the voices around me and studying the curtain, floor, sheets, monitors, signs, tubes, sink, and medicine cabinet in my small cubicle.

Another hour passed, and the curtain surrounding the bed moved aside. An oh-so-very-welcome visitor appeared, and with her, a momentary respite from my oppressive fear.

"Are you still having pain?" asked a nurse. Cheerful little animals hung from her stethoscope.

"Yes," I said, and instinctively placed my hand over my heart. "Using one to ten, with ten being unbearable, how bad is it?" she asked.

"It's a seven," I answered.

"Seven. It's a seven," I repeated to myself as the nurse made handwritten notes on the chart that hung from the bottom of my bed. I had been in the hospital for several hours now, taking regular doses of nitroglycerin tablets. My blood pressure and pulse were now lower, my heart was beating regularly, but the pain was still there: silent, strong, a force in its own right.

"Here," said the nurse as I glanced down and noticed she was wearing Bugs Bunny socks under her black clogs. "Put this under your tongue. Let's try some more nitroglycerin and see if we can make you more comfortable," she said as she moved me to the spillover section of the ER, where less urgent emergencies were treated.

The tablets the nurse gave me to lower my heart rate gradually dissolved under my tongue. And just as slowly, the regular beep, beep, beep of the heart and blood pressure monitors transformed as flat lines replaced the green, red, yellow, and white peaks on the dark screens.

I imagine the sequence went something like this:

Blood pressure: Stop.

Pulse: Stop.

Heart: Stop.

On a Saturday in September 2005, as I lay on a stretcher in the emergency room of the University of Michigan hospital in Ann Arbor, my heart stopped.

But I lift, float, glide away. I am weightless. Confused because I see my body floating and I feel myself inside it at the same time. I pass through a doorway to a foggy place. I know I am thinking, but I can't see.

I am calm and surprised but not scared.

In fact, the opposite is true. It feels really good where I am. An indescribable peace comes as I welcome this new reality.

No pulse, no heartbeat, but I am somewhere. In the "in between."

I'm floating. I can see my body below me on the stretcher, but I am not in it. It feels good where I am now. Soft. Safe. Quiet. I guess I don't have to work so hard anymore.

But I thought I'd have more time to enjoy my new life in Ann Arbor—my house, my freedom. I liked being called "Dr. Tracy," but I guess this is it. Hello, death. I'm not scared. It actually feels okay.

Everyone wants to know what it's like when our hearts stop. When our spirits begin to leave our bodies. Where do we go? What does it feel like? And perhaps the ultimate question: Do we live one life in a body, and that's it? I can't answer those questions. I only know what it was like for me. I now believe I was moving through a space when something pulled me back.

I stopped the forward progression of my consciousness and made the most important decision in my life: I chose to stay in my body.

I believe the force that pulled me back exists inside and outside of me. Some might call it atman, monad, soul, or divinity. I discovered and negotiated that power: exerted my free will while swimming in what I believe is the all, the energy of love.

As the force that drew me out of my body pulled me gently onward to that next plane of existence, I protested: *I can't leave now. There's no one in Michigan to take care of Mike. I can't leave*, I repeated to whoever was listening.

And someone was listening.

That was the first, last, and only thought that registered firmly in my mind as I dropped down what felt like an empty elevator—no elegance, grace, or gentle floating. Someone or something heard my protests, because I landed sharply, abruptly, firmly back into my body with a thud-like plop.

Time started again. Tick, tick, tick. I saw the second hand on the big, round clock on the wall. I heard the familiar beep, beep, beep of the monitors.

A new life. A new birthday. A new beginning, with the realization that there is more: The physical plane isn't all there is. There is somewhere we go when our bodies die, and here's the most important piece:

We are in choice.

That's the most important part of my story that you need to understand.

I have a new and profound respect for those who understand that there is something beyond this human existence, because I saw: I went to the other side, to another place, to the eternal everlasting. Amen. I had a near-death experience while being treated for symptoms of a heart attack at the University of Michigan's hospital in Ann Arbor. I left my body and came to the profound understanding that we are always in choice.

"You scared us," said a doctor who was simultaneously looking at my face and the monitors. A nurse then rolled my bed into a busier place in the ER where they could check on me more frequently. I stared at the fluorescent lights above my head and reflected on how I'd been living my life.

I was grateful that I did not have many regrets.

My brush with death showed me that it was my connection to the all—the force that creates, moves, and unites everything throughout universes, which manifested in my deep love for my sons—that offered me the choice to stay in my body.

The word "love" is often casually used, diminishing the profound connection that is possible between and among humans. Union and commitment better describe the bond that can exist, and the work that is required to build it.

How would my life have been different if I had known this earlier? I spent a lot of my life fighting the reality of my existence, trying to figure things out, wishing things—especially me—were different.

Would I have suffered less if I had tasted the eternal as a young girl?

After passing out from the pain of having stitches removed in college, when I recovered consciousness I was told I had to suffer if I wanted to go to heaven. My childhood faith taught me that suffering on earth prepared one for the afterlife: Heaven was the destination after a virtuous life.

Teilhard taught me that our work is here, and heaven is here too. Leaving and returning to my body cemented my understanding that we are not the circumstances of our lives: We are not our bodies; we are more.

We are all "pilgrims of the future" able to direct evolution through conscious choice.

Ten

The future, however, is finer than any past.
That, as you know, is what I firmly believe.

—Pierre Teilhard de Chardin, *The Making of a Mind*

ON A SUNNY THURSDAY, I left my home in Boulder, Colorado, for the hundredth anniversary celebration of Teilhard's "The Mass on the World," the poetic masterpiece he wrote on the Ordos desert near the border of Mongolia in 1923.

It was October of 2023: Close to forty years had passed since I first encountered the Jesuit priest, and the power of our connection had stayed strong.

The timing of the event was eerie; the liturgy was the day after my fiftieth high school reunion in New Jersey and an easy stop on my way north to visit my son Brendan in Schenectady and my friend Michael Halloran in Troy.

I felt Teilhard taking my hand and guiding me.

Rain changed the location of the ceremony from Teilhard's grave on the Culinary Institute of America's campus to a nearby retreat center. I decided to go first to the Jesuit cemetery to spend a few moments alone with the spirit of my beloved mentor.

I was getting direction from another voice, too; my rental car's Apple CarPlay gave me precise, real-time guidance so I could relax and enjoy the journey. Time passed quickly, and I was soon crossing the Mid-Hudson Bridge, a route I regularly took in the '80s when I worked at Marist College in Poughkeepsie.

Driving past Marist prepared me for the changes that time brings. As I pulled onto the campus of the Culinary Institute a few miles north of the college, I thought about the first time I physically connected with Teilhard. It was in 2011, when I was doing research in the Georgetown archives and read his letters.

Some were in English and some in French. I remember carefully picking up a thin piece of onion skin and staring at the date and signature. I took a breath, slowed down my brain, and brought myself fully into the moment: I was holding a letter Teilhard wrote, typed, and signed with his own hand. Inside the next manila folder was a large black and white picture of Teilhard in silhouette. I held the picture in my hand and stared at three men standing at the entrance of a deep cave.

That's when the tears came. Leaky, wet tears that dripped down my face.

In that small, dark room in the basement of the Georgetown library, I felt safe to let something deep and mysterious flow from inside me, bypassing my brain and connecting directly with my heart.

A knock interrupted my musing: It was the archivist returning to check on me.

"How are you doing?" he asked.

"I wish I knew French. A lot of the letters are in English, but there is so much I couldn't read," I said.

"Would you like to see a video of Teilhard in China? It's short and grainy, but I believe it is one of the only actual films we have of him," he said.

"Yes. Certainly," I said as I helped him set up a small machine on a wooden table in another room in the library.

He left me alone to watch a tall man with a long nose and big smile climb into a low boat on a rocky shore. I watched Pierre Teilhard de Chardin, my guiding light, turn and wave to his friends as he floated down a shallow river.

How had this skinny Frenchman come to mean so much to me? And what had changed since I first stood at his grave?

I was about to get an answer.

The slap of the windshield wipers and the green-and-gold Culinary Institute of America sign jolted me back to the present. I drove through the Institute campus and marveled at the changes since my last visit: Elegant and aesthetically beautiful buildings graced the busy campus where young people worked hard to become accomplished chefs.

I parked my car and followed a winding, wooded path to the security office.

"Can I get the key to the Jesuit cemetery?" I asked the guard.

She nodded politely, so I asked the same question I had asked years ago: "How many people visit Teilhard's grave each day?"

"Oh, we have one or two groups," she answered.

It's groups now. Not just one or two people. I let her answer simmer in my consciousness as I walked to the cemetery, which was now much easier to find because the parking lot had grown close to the iron gate surrounding it.

I rested my small striped umbrella on the ground, put the shiny key into the large padlock that opened the gate, and walked inside.

Arrived.

And gratefully alone.

An air of serenity enveloped me as I walked east toward the river, where the cluster of white headstones sat in neat rows lightly covered with a envelope of moss.

Where was he? I initially felt lost as I searched, but I quickly recalled that his grave was lovingly cared for and adorned with seasonal plantings by a small group of gray-haired women with shining faces who my friend Frank Frost affectionately called "the grave ladies."

I noticed the rust and yellow mums first, and slowly walked in the gentle rain to the shiny white stone that seemed to glow amid the beauty of the quiet glen. I put my arms around the stone and talked to Teilhard in the language of my heart.

I heard his words in my head: "Just trust life."

I sent my spirit to the place where I felt Teilhard's presence and asked him to send me a gift of guidance.

"You know everything you need to know. Now it's time to share. Share, and remember I am human like you," was his message.

I touched the small rock that rested on the top of the headstone with the words *Always Remember* etched into it. I stood at the grave not wanting to leave, but knowing my time was short if I was to join in the anniversary celebration nearby.

I vowed to share the truths inside me and reluctantly left the grave, returned the key, drove north to the retreat center, and arrived on time to see a small cluster of mostly gray-haired French people milling about.

I greeted my hosts Frank and Mary Frost, joined the procession, and was invited to sit where I could easily watch the singing, dancing, and recitation of Teilhard's liturgical poetry in French and English.

As if hundreds of knitting needles were weaving threads of joy, desire, and affection in my heart, I was swept away by the energy of Teilhard's words resurrected anew by devotees from around the world gathered at the beloved priest's final resting place.

Marie Bayon de la Tour, Teilhard's great-niece, read a meticulously researched chronology of the end of Teilhard's life in New York City that captured both his mental anguish and his desire to be remembered. Just a month before his death, he wrote of his longing: "To continue tenaciously to write with the idea that others will eventually see what I see, if I manage to see it myself clearly and intensely enough."

As the liturgy ended, I turned to face those close to me to offer a gesture of peace. I did not know their names, but I felt their hearts and especially their joy.

We were no longer strangers.

This is Teilhard's omega: love as an evolutionary force.

I am inextricably linked across time and place to this mystical soldier-priest-scientist, who not only understood the mysteries of the universe, but lived their practical message.

He knew why we are here.

And now, I know.

Just trust Life:
Life will bring you high,
if only you are careful in selecting,
in the maze of events, those influences or those paths
which can bring you each time
a little more upward.
Life has to be discovered
and built step by step:
a great charm,
if only one is convinced
(by faith and experience)
that the world is going somewhere.

Pierre Teilhard de Chardin, *Letters to Two Friends*

Notes

Prologue   "We are not human beings having a spiritual experience...": This popular quote is often attributed to Teilhard, but it does not appear in any of his published writing. According to the American Teilhard Association (https://teilharddechardin. org), this "quotation" attributed to Teilhard "can be considered a paraphrase of Hegel's dictum that matter is spirit fallen into a state of self-otherness."

One   "All around us, tangibly and materially...": Pierre Teilhard de Chardin, *The Future of Man* (Harper & Row, 1964), 125.

"Teilhard coined the word 'noosphere' in 1922...": Christine M. Tracy. "Teilhard de Chardin and a Technology of Grace," 2009. *EME, the Journal of the Media Ecology Association* 8, no. 2 (2009): 139.

"Like a dance, he saw these two forces...": The relationship of the interior of the collective and Teilhard's noosphere is described by Carter Phipps in *Evolutionaries*. 2012. (HarperCollins, 2012), 164–65.

"WWI, the infamous 'war to end all wars' ": This description is taken from the 1914 book by H. G. Wells *The War That Will End War*. Nadège Mougel, "World War I casualties,"https://www.portvillehistory.org/files/REPERES_module_1-1-1_-_explanatory_notes_World_War_I_casualties_EN.pdf

"The center of perspective...": Pierre Teilhard de Chardin, *The Human Phenomenon* (Sussex Academic Press, 1999), 4.

Two   "By virtue of the biological quality...": Pierre Teilhard de Chardin, *The Human Phenomenon* (Sussex Academic Press, 1999), 4.

"...in 1928 when a Jesuit traveled...": Amir D. Aczel, *The Jesuit and the Skull: Teilhard de Chardin, Evolution, and the Search for the Peking Man* (Riverhead Books, 2007), 128.

"A bird being whirled about...": Pierre Teilhard de Chardin, letter to Valensin, January 10, 1926, cited in Robert Speaight, *Teilhard de Chardin—A Biography* (Collins, 1967), 140.

Three   "It often happens that...": Pierre Teilhard de Chardin, *The Human Phenomenon* (Sussex Academic Press, 1999), 3.

Four   "...the front cannot but attract us...": Pierre Teilhard de Chardin, *The Making of a Mind: Letters from a Soldier-Priest 1914–1919* (Harper & Row, 1965), 205.

"...the center of construction...": Pierre Teilhard de Chardin, *The Human Phenomenon* (Sussex Academic Press, 1999), 4.

"...the entire fraction of the cosmos...": Pierre Teilhard de Chardin, *The Human Phenomenon* (Sussex Academic Press, 1999), 4.

"And if we are to be happy—completely happy,...": Pierre Teilhard de Chardin, *On Happiness* (Collins, 1973), 54–55.

"...ever more perfect eyes...": Pierre Teilhard de Chardin, *The Human Phenomenon* (Sussex Academic Press, 1999), 3.

Five   "What paralyzes life...": Pierre Teilhard de Chardin, *On Love & Happiness* (Harper & Row), 15–16.

"...Truth has to appear only once...": Pierre Teilhard de Chardin, "The Christic," in *The Heart of the Matter* (Harcourt, 1978), 102.

"the modernists' understanding..." https://en.wikipedia.org/wiki/Scopes_trial

"His superiors ordered Teilhard...": David Grumett, "Teilhard, the Six Propositions, and Human Origins: A Response," *Zygon Journal of Science and Religion* 54, no. 4 (2019): 954–964, https://onlinelibrary.wiley.com/doi/10.1111/zygo.12552

"The Chinese had a special name...": Ursula King, *Spirit of Fire: The Life and Vision of Teilhard de Chardin* (Orbis Books, 1996), 133.

Six   "The day will come...": Pierre Teilhard de Chardin, "The Evolution of Chastity," in *On Love & Happiness* (The Great Library Collection, R.P. Pryne, 2015), 5.

"We are quite naturally impatient...": Pierre Teilhard de Chardin, "Patient Trust," in *Hearts on Fire: Praying with Jesuits*, ed. Michael Harter (Loyola Press, 1993), 102.

Seven   "What would we do without our enemies? ": Pierre Teilhard de Chardin, *The Human Phenomenon* (Sussex Academic Press, 1999), 97.

"...you seem to feel...": Pierre Teilhard de Chardin, "Nostalgia for the Front," in *The Heart of Matter* (Harcourt, 1978), 167.

Eight   "I incline to believe that...": Pierre Teilhard de Chardin, *Letters to Leontine Zanta* (Harper & Row, 1969), 91.

"What paralyzes life is...": Pierre Teilhard de Chardin, *On Love & Happiness* (Harper & Row, 1984), 15–16.

Nine "Love is the most universal...": Pierre Teilhard de
      Chardin, "Spirit of the Earth," in *Human Energy*
      (Harcourt Brace Jovanovich, 1969), 32–34.

Ten   "The future, however, is finer...": Pierre Teilhard de
      Chardin, letter, September 5, 1919, in *The Making
      of a Mind, Letters from a Soldier-Priest 1914–1919*
      (Harper & Row, 1965), 306.

      "Just trust life...": Pierre Teilhard de Chardin, *Letters
      to Two Friends, 1926–1952* (New American Library,
      1939), 127.

      "To continue tenaciously to write...": Marie Bayon de
      la Tour, quotation from Pierre Teilhard de Chardin's
      unpublished diary entry dated March 13, 1955, in
      "The End of Pierre Teilhard de Chardin's life in New
      York," Poughkeepsie, New York, Saturday, October
      21, 2023.

      "Just trust Life...": Pierre Teilhard de Chardin, Letters
      to Two Friends, 1926–1952, cited in Blanche
      Gallagher, *Meditations with Teilhard de Chardin*
      (Bear & Co., 1988), 142.

Acknowledgments

I feel the energy of the guiding lights in my life as I launch this book into the world.

I'll start with Carol Metz, who hired me at the Culinary Institute of America where I first discovered Pierre Teilhard de Chardin. Next is John December, who assigned the essay that brought Teilhard back into my life. "Teilhard is an ethos worth exploring," wrote my beloved friend Michael Halloran, a continuing source of encouragement and support.

A special thank you to Marianne Simpson, who encouraged me to keep writing about Teilhard. I took your advice.

So much gratitude for friends and colleagues in the Media Ecology Association and the Integral Theory and Developmental Philosophy communities, especially

Steve McIntosh: Thank you for creating the ripples of resonance which kept me afloat and looking forward.

I am grateful for the passionate mission and ongoing work of the American Teilhard Association. A special thank you to Frank and Mary Frost for your exquisite documentary *Teilhard: Visionary Scientist* and for the Teilhard Project. We are forever joined in the joy of bringing Teilhard's message forward.

All the beautiful women in my writing communities helped me get to this moment. I started working on this book in Tanja Pajevic's Lighthouse Writers Workshop in 2019 and then her Memoir Mastermind group. My "badass writing coach" Chris Chandler and my writing group members Cait McQuade and Jennifer Rhode lovingly listened and held my hand through the hard parts. So grateful to Lisa Jones for your amazing workshops, especially "Seven Scenes in Seven Weeks."

Thank you to the Daredevil writers: Nicole Harkin, Cindy Powell, Jessica Goldmuntz Stokes, Chris Chandler, and Sandi Phinney for giving me space, encouragement, and advice.

Then there is my special angel, Anne Heaton. Thank you for being you and for our friendship. Your courage, creativity, and spirit inspire me.

My heart is full of gratitude for my dear sons Mike and Brendan, who stood by me as I lived my life. A big thank you to my daughter-in-law Brooke for your friendship and love. I am gifted with four glorious grandchildren, Wade, Owen, Genesis, and Grace; you are my joy and my legacy. May my words bring you comfort and ease when you need it most.

Thank you, John. You witnessed the unfolding and patiently watched me log hours, days, months, and years at my desk. True love.

I am deeply appreciative of Lilly Dancyger's developmental edit and Alisson Wood's coaching. A special thank you to my friends Michael Halloran and Katya Haskins for your early reads and encouragement, and to Nic Sims for your expert advice and support.

Thank you, thank you, thank you, dear Natalie Tomlin. You lifted me up, dusted me off, set me on the right path, and guided me along the way with your special blend of gentle and insightful editing. I am so proud of what we have done together. And to Raúl, for capturing the essence of the book on the cover and inside. It feels transcendent.

May the magic continue....

Christine M. Tracy
November 5, 2024

www.ingramcontent.com/pod-product-compliance
Lightning Source LLC
Chambersburg PA
CBHW031529120626
46545CB00005B/2068